For
Believers
Only

For Believers Only

J. OSWALD SANDERS

DIMENSION BOOKS
BETHANY FELLOWSHIP, INC.
Minneapolis, Minn. 55438

For Believers Only
By J. Oswald Sanders

Published in 1976 by Bethany Fellowship, Inc., by special arrangement with Zondervan Publishing House, Grand Rapids, Mich.

Library of Congress Catalog Card Number 76-15347
ISBN 0-87123-161-1

Copyright © 1972 by J. Oswald Sanders

Published in England by Marshall, Morgan & Scott under the title *The World's Greatest Sermon*

Published in the United States by Zondervan Publishing House under the title *Real Discipleship*

DIMENSION BOOKS
Published by Bethany Fellowship, Inc.
6820 Auto Club Road, Minneapolis, Minn. 55438

Printed in the United States of America

Contents

I

Introduction

Matthew 5 : 1–2

This book aims to provide a popular devotional exposition of the Sermon on the Mount. Some readers who are interested mainly in the exposition itself may prefer to skip this introductory chapter and begin directly with the study of the Beatitudes in Chapter 2. But there are important problems raised by the Sermon which demand explanation, although they may be less interesting. The introductory material, however, throws much light on Christ's teaching and its correct interpretation.

In essence, the Sermon constitutes a portrait of the Preacher Himself—'not the lines of a legal code, but the lineaments of a character'. The perfectly balanced character of our Lord Jesus Christ resulted from the diligent practice of His own precepts. He lived what He taught. If conformity to His own teaching produced so strong and attractive a Person as He, we are encouraged to expect that a similar conformity on our part will result in a radical transformation in us.

KEYS TO INTERPRETATION

In the interpretation of the Sermon several factors must be taken into account if we are to discover its inner meaning.

Its genius lies in the fact that, rather than promulgating a series of rules for the spiritual life, it lays down great and far-reaching spiritual *principles*. The scribes and Pharisees had so cluttered the Mosaic Law with petty restrictions and regulations that it had become an intolerable burden to the devout Jew. Jesus aimed in His teaching to remedy this crushing legalism.

Much of the Sermon is couched in *poetical* form. Such poetical passages cannot, therefore, be interpreted according to the canons of plain prose. This is one reason why a rigidly literal interpretation only serves to complicate rather than interpret some passages. Poetical passages are to be interpreted as poetry.

The Oriental cast of mind generally makes it easier for them to appreciate concrete illustrations of truth than to grasp abstract ideas. Where we say, 'In the Lord is everlasting strength', they would say, 'The Lord is the rock of ages' (Isa. 26 : 4 Berkeley). As the Master Teacher, our Lord therefore adopted the *parabolic* method of instruction. His teaching is studded with colourful illustrations from contemporary life. In the Sermon He employs no fewer than forty-eight figures of speech.

He also used the *proverbial* method of teaching which appeals so much to the Oriental even in our day. A proverb is an extreme and hyperbolical method of conveying truth. The parable of the mote and beam in the Sermon is a case in point. The hyperbole in the parable serves to highlight more vividly the folly and blindness which allow us to criticise in others faults of which we are doubly guilty ourselves.

Since the Sermon is cast in this rather complex form, we must avoid grotesque and wooden literalism in our interpretation or we will find ourselves arriving at absurd conclusions.

An obvious example is the Lord's command to pluck out our right eye if it provides an occasion of stumbling or leading us into temptation. Even if we were courageous enough to render literal obedience would the same temptation not be able to enter through the left eye? Obviously the correct interpretation must lie in another direction.

Insistence on an absolutely literal interpretation of the Sermon, altogether irrespective of whether it is given as poetry, parable or proverb, can result only in obscuring the truth Jesus was endeavouring to reveal. On the other hand, we must avoid the opposite peril of robbing it of its pungency and point by an undue spiritualising of its language.

TWO SERMONS OR ONE?

The differences between Luke's record of the Sermon and that of Matthew are so considerable as to demand some comment (cf. Luke 6 with Matt. 5–7).

While the two accounts have a great deal of material in common, there appear to be some significant differences. Of the 107 verses in Mathew's account, only thirty appear in Luke's record. Luke has four passages which have no parallel in Matthew (Luke 6:24–6, 27, 34, 35, 37, 38). One suggested solution to the problem—that Luke gives an epitome of Matthew's account—is difficult to substantiate. If Luke aimed to give a condensed report, how explain the fact that in several verses Luke's account, instead of being briefer, is fuller than that of Matthew?

One popular view is that Matthew was not recording a set discourse delivered on one occasion, but rather compiled a compendium of Jesus's sayings spoken at intervals during His ministry, but edited by him as if they were delivered at one time. This view makes either one or both of the accounts entirely unhistorical, and this is inadmissible.

A modification of the above view is that Jesus went up the mountain to pray, and chose His disciples. He then taught them over a period, and the Sermon is a digest of the teaching He gave on that occasion (Luke 6:11, 12).

Against this view it should be noted that the whole discourse commences with the words. 'And he opened his mouth and taught them, saying . . .' It concludes with the words, 'And it came to pass when Jesus had ended these sayings . . .' (5:2; 7:28). Would this not give the impression to an ordinary reader that he had before him a connected discourse, and not a collection of largely unrelated sayings?

In the light of all the facts it would seem that two views are tenable, neither of which would do violence to the text or teaching of the Sermon.

The first, advocated by J. Russell Howden,[1] holds that the discourses reported by Matthew and Luke are entirely separate and distinct. This would not be improbable, for it is most likely that Jesus repeated His teaching concerning the laws of the Kingdom not once, but many times, as He addressed different groups in different centres. When we repeat ourselves we do not necessarily do so in identical words, nor need He have done so. On each occasion the Sermon would embody peculiarities of its own, while presenting the same general line of truth.

The other view, held by so eminent a scholar as Professor A. T. Robertson,[2] maintains that the discourses of Matthew and Luke are the same, and that there are no insuperable problems in reconciling the apparent differences. Both accounts begin and end alike, and pursue the same general order. Luke omits various matters of special interest to Jewish readers, e.g. Matt. 5:17–42, and other material which he himself purposed to give later, e.g. 11:1–4; 12:22, 27).

The superficial problem posed by the fact that Matthew speaks of the discourse being delivered on a mountain, while Luke affirms it was spoken on a level place, is not difficult of solution. Both could be true; Luke could have been referring to a level plateau on

Matthew's mountain. If, as tradition has it, the Horns of Hattin, a mountain not far from Capernaum, was the venue of the Sermon, there is just such a plateau between the two peaks or 'horns'. It would provide an eminently suitable amphitheatre for a large crowd.

In presenting factors in support of the view that the two accounts are identical and refer to the same occasion, William Hendriksen[3] shows that the historical setting is the same in both Gospels. It is preceded by the account of the multitude flocking to Jesus for healing, and followed by the healing of the centurion's servant. The train of thought is the same in both accounts. It appears as a coherent discourse, a complete message, evidencing an inner unity. The writers apparently intend to give the impression that all the sayings were spoken at one time.

The differences in the two accounts are explicable on the basis that Matthew had one group of readers in mind, while Luke had another, and this affected the material each presented. Matthew had Jews especially in mind, and therefore included more material directly relevant to the Pharisees' misinterpretations of the Mosaic Law (5:17–6:18).

TO WHOM SPOKEN?

> And seeing the *multitudes*, he went up into a mountain: and when he was set his *disciples* came unto him: and he opened his mouth and *taught them* ... (5:1, 2).

The great crowds that thronged Jesus formed the background of His audience. In a close circle around Him was the small band of His recently chosen disciples, the Inner Circle through whom He purposed to mediate His gospel to the whole world.

The record makes it clear that Jesus spoke the message to His disciples who came to Him, but with the crowd listening in. Bishop Gore puts it felicitously : 'The Sermon on the Mount was spoken in the ear of the church, and overheard by the world.'

That our Lord's teaching was intended *indirectly* for the world is borne out by the closing words of the Sermon, 'When Jesus ended these sayings, *the people* were astonished at his doctrine, for he taught them as one having authority.' The Lord *sees* the crowd, He *teaches* the Church, for it is through His disciples that He reaches out into society.

In view of what has been written it would seem justifiable to conclude that the Sermon was not for non-Christians, but for believers; not for nations as such, but for individuals; not only for believers in a coming day, but for every disciple today.

SOME MISCONCEPTIONS

When views are strongly held the suggestion of apparent weaknesses in these views is not always welcomed. In discussing some currently held views which do not seem to him tenable it is the author's endeavour to do so with Christian charity and yet with faithfulness to the text as he sees it.

The Idealistic View

To some, the Sermon is a beautiful ideal to be admired and praised, but quite unrealistic and irrelevant in the kind of world in which we live today. It has its value in days of falling standards as a counsel of perfection, but is quite beyond the possibility of our practical emulation or attainment.

But this view is negatived by such a statement as : 'Therefore you are to be perfect, as your heavenly Father is perfect' (5:48 N.A.S.V.). There is no scaling down of God's command to the level of man's weakness and failure here. God does not demand the impossible of us, and the exact significance of the verse which will appear in the exposition, shows that it is capable of attainment.

God's truth is eternal, and the unchanging principles enunciated by the Lord in the Sermon are of perennial application and appropriateness. While we do not possess the inherent resources to live up to so demanding a standard, God provides the dynamic for obedience.

The Liberal Theological View

To many modern theologians the Sermon on the Mount is the distilled essence of Christianity. It contains all we need to know for Christian living. Not divisive doctrine, but ethics is its key note. The offensive blood-theology is marked by its absence. It holds out the promise of eternal life to the individual and prosperity to the nation. If only the principles of the Sermon were adopted by the nations, peace and prosperity would be assured.

An able answer to this view has been given by Harrington C. Lees : [4]

> We find that, so far from the Sermon on the Mount having no dogmatic presuppositions, and no evangelical foundations—instead of ignoring incarnation and divine Sonship, free pardon and spiritual fullness—that it assumes as axiomatic the divinity of the human Christ, the royal position of Him who is both Son of David and Son of God, the one approach for the sinner by repentance and faith, and for the cleansed soul—the power of the Holy Spirit to enable him for conquest in private walk . . . As Dr Dale has finely said, 'The ethics of the Sermon on the Mount have their root in the mystical relations between Christ and His people.'

In negation of this viewpoint is the fact that Jesus gave this teaching to His disciples, who had already entered the Kingdom of God; and it was His clear and consistent teaching that this was possible only through the experience of new birth (John 3:3, 5). Neither directly nor by implication is the teaching of the Sermon held out as a way to salvation and eternal life for the unbelieving man. Jesus demanded of citizens of His Kingdom a change of heart and life so radical that it could be compared only to a new birth.

Nor is adoption of the principles enunciated in the Sermon held out as a panacea that will bring peace and prosperity to nations. That the level of national life would be greatly raised if citizens practised these principles is undoubtedly true, but the mere adoption of Christ's ethical standards does not qualify for entrance into the Kingdom of God.

The Dispensational View

In various forms and with peripheral differences, it is affirmed by godly Bible teachers that the teaching of the Sermon on the Mount is not valid for Christians in this age or dispensation. The view was popularised by Dr C. I. Scofield, and gained wide credence in evangelical circles through his widely-known Reference Bible.

In a note[5] he makes this assertion : 'For these reasons, the Sermon on the Mount in its primary application gives *neither the duty nor the privilege of the Church*. These are found in the Epistles.' But as will be shown later, the Sermon is the seed-plot of the teaching in the Epistles, and every principle stated in the Sermon is re-iterated in one form or another in the Epistles.

He goes on to concede that 'there is a beautiful moral application to the Christian'. To exponents of this view, in its more extreme form at least, the real validity of the teaching of the Sermon is postponed to a future 'Kingdom age', for 'the remnant' to whom it will be appropriate. The logical corollary of this proposition is that Christians today need feel no sense of condemnation if they do not conform to the demands of the Sermon, since it defines 'neither the privilege nor the duty of the Church' of today.

But does not this line of teaching have serious implications in our attitude to the Scriptures? The sincerity of those who hold this position is not in doubt, nor is it suggested that there is any intentional dishonour to the Lord or His Word, but it does have serious and important implications. While the inspiration and authority of the passage are not impugned, *practically* this influential passage is denied to the Church for its whole history up to this time, and is reserved for the few who will be alive in the 'the Kingdom age'.

It is not to be wondered at that Charles F. Hogg,[6] a noted expositor of the Open Brethren, himself a premillennialist in his theology, in his commentary wrote: 'The dispensational key effects the mutilation of the Sermon rather than its interpretation.' G. C. D. Howley recently wrote:

> It is sad that some have misled Christians concerning the force of the Sermon on the Mount; some have suggested that it is Jewish teaching. There is no foundation whatever for this approach, nor could it ever have been recorded as valid had its exponents not first set the Gospel by Matthew within their own special framework. Once this was done, then everything—whatever the text may say —had to be interpreted in the light of that presupposition. Had there been even a whisper in the words of Jesus that He did not intend this teaching for the persons in front of Him, then there might have been grounds for this theory. But without one word to suggest that He did not intend the teaching for them, we become seriously in danger of divorcing Christ's teaching from reality.[7]

When in this same Gospel our Lord commanded His disciples, 'Go ye therefore, and teach all nations

15

. . . teaching them to observe all things whatsoever I have commanded you . . .' (28 : 20), have we any scriptural or logical grounds for believing that this extended passage was excluded from the terms of His commission?

If it be objected that the ethics of the Sermon are law and not grace, would the answer not be that the primary purpose of grace is to enable us to meet the demands of God's holy law? Paul asserts that the purpose of the incarnation was 'that the righteousness of the law might be fulfilled in us' (Rom. 8 : 4).

In point of fact it is this very ethical teaching which is one of the Church's greatest needs in our day. Moral and ethical standards have plummetted to their nadir, and the voice of our Lord through His Church sorely needs to be heard. Let us not allow anyone, whether liberal or evangelical in their theological views, and however sincere in their personal convictions, to deprive us of the challenge, the searching, and the inspiration of this matchless Sermon.

MODE OF TEACHING

> And seeing the multitudes, he went up into a mountain: and when he was set, his disciples came to him, and he opened his mouth and taught them saying . . . (5 : 1, 2).

When a rabbi was teaching officially it was his custom to sit down. At other times he might teach while strolling about, as Jesus did on many of His journeys. The fact that He sat down to deliver this Sermon indicates that He regarded it in the light of an important official pronouncement.

The importance of the occasion was heightened by the words, 'and he opened his mouth'. This phrase was used only of solemn, grave language and weighty sayings. It was employed to describe utterances in which

16

one dropped all barriers and opened one's heart to the hearers.

The fact that the verb 'taught', in the clause 'and he taught them', is in the imperfect tense, conveys the thought of repeated or habitual action; hence, 'he used to teach them'. This has been cited in support of the view that Jesus repeated this teaching to different groups.

The standards of the Sermon are desperately high, and seem hopelessly idealistic to us earthy men, but we must not forget that the Sermon is set side by side with a living example. It was the exemplification of the life which Jesus had lived both in obscurity and in the glare of publicity. And it had already been affirmed of Him who preached it, that He came to save us from our sins (1:21) and to provide the dynamic for abundant living.

WHAT IS THE KINGDOM OF HEAVEN?

To answer this question adequately would take much more space than is available, so we will deal with a large subject very briefly.

Some expositors see a distinction between the Kingdom of God and the Kingdom of heaven, but it is generally agreed that in the New Testament the two terms seem to be used interchangeably, perhaps with some difference of emphasis (cf. Matt. 4:17 with Mark 1:14).

The word 'kingdom' can have three meanings: (1) The realm over which a king reigns. (2) The people over whom a king reigns. (3) The actual reign or rule itself— and this latter is the primary meaning of the word. Hence, 'the Kingdom of heaven' means the reign of God in heart and life. The Church is composed of men and women who acknowledge the sovereignty of God.

The phrase is sometimes used in an abstract sense, as in Mark 10:15. It is those who 'receive the kingdom of God as a little child', i.e. accept the rule of God in their lives here and now, who enter into its future blessings.

1. In the *Sunday School Times*, 25th December, 1926, p. 791.

2. A. T. Robertson, *Word Pictures in the New Testament* (New York, Harper, 1930), p. 38.

3. William Hendriksen, *The Sermon on the Mount* (Grand Rapids, Eerdmans), p. 29.

4. Harrington C. Lees, *The King's Way* (London, Marshall Brothers), p. 11.

5. The Scofield Reference Bible, p. 1000.

6. Hogg and Vine, *The Sermon on the Mount* (London, Pickering and Inglis).

7. *Life of Faith*, 11th April, 1970, p. 7.

2

Analysis of the Sermon on the Mount

INTRODUCTORY 5:1–2

THE SOURCE OF THE DISCIPLE'S JOY—THE BEATITUDES
5:3–12

> The first group—passive personal qualities 3–6
> The second group—active social qualities 7–12

THE SAVOUR OF THE DISCIPLE'S WITNESS 5:13–16

> Salt—the pungency of the disciple 13
> Light—the radiance of the disciple 14a
> A city set on a hill—the prominence of the disciple
> 14b–16

THE SACREDNESS OF THE DIVINE REVELATION 5:17–20

> Attitude to prior revelation 17
> The perpetuity of the Law 18–20

THE SPIRITUALITY OF THE DISCIPLE'S ATTITUDES
5:21–48

> Self-control versus forbidden anger 21–6
> Moral purity versus forbidden desire 27–32

Simple truthfulness versus forbidden swearing 33–7

Non-retaliation versus forbidden vengeance 38–42

Impartial love versus forbidden hatred 43–5

THE SINCERITY OF THE DISCIPLE'S MOTIVE 6:1–18

Secrecy versus forbidden ostentation 1

Almsgiving—generosity to one's neighbour 2–4

Prayer—devotion to God 5–15

Fasting—discipline of self 16–18

THE SECRETS OF THE DISCIPLE'S PRAYER 6:9–13

The invocation 9

The petitions—concerning God and his glory 9–10

The petitions—concerning man and his needs 11–13

The doxology

THE SIMPLICITY OF THE DISCIPLE'S POSSESSIONS 6:19–24

Treasure on earth 19

Treasure in heaven 20–1

Single vision 22–3

Single service 24

THE SERENITY OF THE DISCIPLE'S TRUST 6:25–34

The forbidden worry 25

Worry is needless 26

Worry is futile 27–9

Worry is faithless 30–1

Worry is pagan 32

Faith's priority 33–4

3

The Source of the Disciple's Joy

Matthew 5:3–12

> On the first reading of the Sermon on the Mount you feel it turns everything upside down, but the second time you read it, you discover that it turns everything right side up. The first time you read it you feel that it is impossible, but the second time, you feel that nothing else is possible.

So G. K. Chesterton expressed the sense of paradox that must impress anyone who reads this imperial sermon of the ages seriously. For example, Jesus promulgates the manifesto of His Kingdom with an eight-fold promise of blessedness. 'Blessed . . . blessed . . . blessed . . .', but then He proceeds to tell His bewildered audience that the pathway along which this bliss will reach them is one of poverty, mourning, hunger, thirst, renunciation, persecution! And this element of paradox persists throughout the whole Sermon. Our Lord's teaching was so unorthodox, so penetrating, so challenging, that there was little danger of His hearers falling asleep.

The Keynote of the Kingdom
It is a popular conception that if only we had wealth, absence of sorrow, unrestricted gratification of appetite, were kindly treated by all, this would be bliss indeed.

22

But Jesus's teaching reversed this entirely. The qualities of character and attitudes of which Jesus said blessedness was the reward, are quite different from what one would expect. The very experiences we are usually most anxious to side-step are the ones most conducive to our joy. In a day when the emphasis is on activism in religion it is rather startling to find our Lord giving so high a rating to passive qualities of character, as He does in the Beatitudes.

In announcing His manifesto it was appropriate that He should begin with its keynote, BLESSED. The word 'are' is not in the original. The opening of each beatitude is really an exclamation, 'O the Bliss of the poor in spirit!' 'Blessed' signifies a deep joy which is independent of the changing circumstances of life, but has the secret of joy in itself. It could be translated, 'superlatively happy', 'to be envied', 'to be congratulated'.

The eight qualities presented in the Beatitudes are a description of one man, the same man, the ideal citizen of the Kingdom in his psychological and spiritual development. There is no thought that the disciple may choose in which of the Beatitudes he will specialise, as for example Moses who was noted for meekness. He is to specialise in them all!

Before studying the Beatitudes in detail it is illuminating to note that the exact opposite of the virtues in the Beatitudes are the qualities which largely distinguish human conduct. In the words of A. W. Tozer[1]

> In the world of men we find nothing approaching the virtues of which Jesus spoke in the opening words of the famous Sermon on the Mount. Instead of poverty of spirit, we find the rankest kind of pride; instead of mourners we find pleasure seekers; instead of meekness, arrogance; instead of hunger after righteousness we hear men saying 'I am rich and increased in goods and have need of nothing; instead of purity of heart, corrupt

imaginations; instead of peacemakers, we find men quarrelsome and resentful; instead of rejoicing in mistreatment, we find them fighting back with every weapon at their command.

The Beatitudes divide into two groups:

The ideal citizen of the Kingdom will be characterised by:

Spiritual Inadequacy

> Blessed are the *poor in spirit*, for theirs is the Kingdom of heaven (v. 3).

Paradoxically, the superlatively happy man is one who is conscious of spiritual inadequacy. 'O the bliss of the inadequate!'

The words 'in spirit' provide the clue to the meaning. There is nothing ethical or blessed in poverty as such. To be poor in spirit does not mean to be poor-spirited. Indeed, the very reverse might well be the case. It is the very antithesis of pride and self-sufficiency. A financially poor man is not automatically poor in spirit. He may be quite as proud and self-sufficient as his rich neighbour.

On one occasion Diogenes visited Plato in his palatial home. Diogenes stamped on the luxurious carpets, saying, 'Thus do I trample underfoot the pride of Plato.' Plato later returned the visit to the house where Diogenes lived in ostentatious poverty. Plato languidly observed that he could see the pride of Diogenes peeping through the holes of his carpet.

Further insight into Jesus's meaning is afforded by the significance of the word 'poor'. Two Greek words are so translated. One means a pauper, the other a beggar. One is poor because of his circumstances and has

24

to work hard to maintain a bare existence. The beggar is poor because he chooses to be poor. He has nothing, and lives on the bounty of others. It is this word that Jesus uses. The truly joyous man is one who is destitute, bankrupt on the grace and bounty of God. Conscious of his need, he looks for help outside himself, and gratefully accepts it.

When Jesus said, 'I can of my own self do nothing', He evinced this poverty of spirit. Paul demonstrated it when he confessed, 'In me, that is in my flesh, dwelleth no good thing.' Proud of his independence and self-sufficiency, the wordly man hates any feeling of inadequacy. The spiritual man, however, in his conscious inadequacy is cast back on the adequacy of God and draws on His illimitable resources. The man of the world often drowns his inadequacy in drink and drugs.

The superlatively happy man is glad to be totally dependent on God, for that is a poverty which leads to spiritual affluence.

Spiritual Contrition

> Blessed are they that *mourn*, for they shall be comforted (v. 4).

The mourning in view here is the sorrow, not of bereavement, but over sin, or perhaps over the pain of others. It is a natural outcome of poverty of spirit. There is no blessedness in the mourning itself. It lies in the comfort promised to those who mourn. Of course, where there is no grief, there can be no comfort.

We again meet paradox. 'O how happy are the unhappy!' We should be on our guard against two misinterpretations of Scripture. One is that Christians should *never* be a laughing, joyous people. Jesus promises no bliss to the moody and morose. It was said anticipatively of the Preacher of the Sermon, 'God hath anointed Thee with the oil of gladness above Thy fellows' (Heb.

1:9). He expects His disciples to be more joyous than their contemporaries, too.

The opposite mistake is that Christians should *always* be laughing. There is a time for mourning in the sense suggested by this beatitude, for no person attains full maturity without the experience of sorrow. Jesus does not overlook the fact that sorrow is the common lot of man.

The primary form of sorrow envisaged here is mourning over one's own sin and spiritual failure. Which of us does not have ample grounds for this? The paucity of our spiritual attainment and slowness of growth in the divine life, our inward depravity or bondage to besetting sin, our unlikeness to Christ, our rebellion against the will of God should give us concern. For any or all of these we should experience a profound sense of regret, sorrow that we have grieved the heart of our Father.

'Mourn' is a strong word, and is used of the passionate lamenting over the dead which accompanied deaths in the East. It expressed the contrition of the penitent Isaiah when he cried : 'Woe is me, for I am undone.' Does it find an echo in our hearts?

Such godly sorrow works repentance, and results in the exchange of the 'oil of joy for the spirit of mourning'. God does not despise the broken and contrite heart, but restores the joy of salvation. It carries with it the assurance of divine comfort, and the wiping away of all tears from our eyes.

Our Lord may also have had in view another form of mourning—mourning that is sympathy with another's pain. It is not difficult to seal ourselves off from the sorrows of those around us, and live in our own hermetically sealed unit. No one will force us to share the griefs and bear the burdens of others. We are not compelled to weep with those who weep, but to do so is a Christian attitude.

The word 'sympathy' means simply, 'to suffer

together with' another, and this could be one aspect of the mourning of which Jesus spoke. 'He bore our griefs and carried our sorrows' sympathetically, as well as bearing our sins vicariously.

Paradoxically this mourning is by no means incompatible with rejoicing. Luke's record gives us this assurance, 'Blessed are ye that weep now, for ye shall laugh' (6:21). Paul experienced both the mourning and the comfort of this beatitude—'sorrowful, yet always rejoicing'.

Spiritual Humility

> Blessed are the *meek*, for they shall inherit the earth (v. 5).

The Psalmist anticipated this beatitude by many centuries, for it is an echo of Psalm 37:11. It is a natural sequence from the previous two, for he who manifests poverty of spirit and mourns over his sinfulness will display a meek and lowly bearing.

Meekness is not mere amiability or mildness of disposition. The meek man will be anything but servile and spineless, for 'meekness is not an invertebrate virtue'. It has nothing whatever in common with the 'umbleness of Uriah Heep, but is the opposite of a haughty and self-assertive spirit.

It is not to be confused with weakness, for 'meek' is a very strong word. It implies forces and strength held in check, under strong control. The word was used of the breaking-in of horses, with the idea of energy controlled, forces of character held firmly in hand.

Reference is made in the book of the Revelation to 'the song of Moses and of the Lamb'. These two are linked together in another significant association. Meekness was an outstanding quality of both, but neither was a milk and water character. Both could blaze in righteous anger. Was Jesus 'gentle and mild' in His

27

treatment of the unholy traffickers in His Father's house of prayer? Yet all the strengths of His character were held on a taut leash.

In this beatitude, Jesus once again challenged and cut across the accepted standards of the world of His day and ours. 'Stand up for your rights', was the prevailing attitude; or in the words of Nietzsche, 'Assert yourself. The world is yours if you can get it.' Jesus rejected this, and said, 'The world is yours if you renounce it! It is the meek not the aggressive who inherit the earth.'

Meekness is the attitude that does not always insist on its own rights, and on having its own way. The meek person will yield to no one where a point of principle is involved, but he will be strong enough to give way when a matter of purely personal advantage is at stake. If he sees an opportunity of advancing the interests of his Master thereby, he will submit to being imposed upon by others.

If injured, he will seek no revenge; if insulted, he will not threaten; if reviled, he will not reciprocate; if treated unjustly, he will not retaliate. It is readily seen that the grace of meekness is a rare, exotic flower, foreign to the smoggy, sooty world in which we live.

Contrary to appearances, the meek man is not 'too good to get on in the world'. It is he who truly inherits the earth. He seeks first the Kingdom of God, and all other necessary things are his too (6:33)—and without any ulcers!

Spiritual Aspiration

> Blessed are they which do *hunger and thirst* after righteousness, for they shall be filled (v. 6).

A sense of spiritual destitution creates desire and aspiration. God is presented in Scripture as almost pathetically eager to satisfy the aspirations of the yearning heart. Abraham Lincoln once wrote, 'I have been reading the Beatitudes, and I can claim at least one of the blessings—the blessing pronounced on those who hunger and thirst after righteousness.'

The Lord uses the elemental instincts of hunger and thirst to convey the idea of passionate desire for holiness. Not mere wistfulness, but insatiable craving. These are two of the most agonising and intense of human appetites. In describing the experiences of his party when they faced extreme and continuous hunger on their polar expedition, Sir Ernest Shackleton said that he and his companions found it difficult to think of anything else than food and eating. This hunger of which Jesus speaks will not be appeased by a light snack or this thirst quenched by a soft drink.

The righteousness which is the focus of the hunger and thirst is not a mere cold conformity to an impersonal law. The objective Jesus had in mind was ethical righteousness, likeness to Himself in outlook and conduct, for is He not 'the Lord our righteousness'? He could therefore have said, with equal truth, 'Blessed are they that hunger and thirst after ME.'

When we cherish an aspiration to likeness to Christ so compelling that it excludes all secondary interests we are already far along the road to satisfaction. This is the beatitude of the insatiably hungry and the unquenchably thirsty.

William Barclay points out that the Greek verbs of hunger and thirst are always followed by the genitive case—'I hunger for of bread', that is, 'I want some bread'. But here it is the accusative case, expressing a longing not for some, but the whole thing, total righteousness.

It is noteworthy that Jesus did not say, 'blessed are they that hunger after *happiness*', which is man's main object of pursuit, but after *righteousness*. The truly joyous man has made the discovery that happiness is a by-product of holiness.

'There is an ignoble pursuit of irresponsible

29

happiness,' said A. W. Tozer. 'Most of us would rather be happy than feel the wounds of other people's sorrow. The holy man will be the useful man, and most likely the happy man too. If he seeks happiness and forgets holiness, he is a carnal man.'

> Then pray for desire, for love's wistfullest yearning,
> For the beautiful pining of holy desire;
> Yes pray for a soul that is ceaselessly burning
> With the soft, fragrant flames of this thrice happy fire.
> F. W. Faber

THE SECOND GROUP—ACTIVE SOCIAL QUALITIES (VV. 7–12)

The ideal citizen of the Kingdom will be :

Compassionate in Spirit

> Blessed are the *merciful*, for they shall obtain mercy (v. 7).

It is possible to have a passion for righteousness, and yet to lack compassion for those who have failed to attain it. Righteousness can be cold and hard and unfeeling and so in this beatitude Jesus speaks of the bliss of the sympathetic.

Mercy can be exercised only to the *undeserving*. If it were deserved, it would not be mercy, but simple justice. In the light of this fact it might prove salutary for us to check our own acts and attitudes and see if we are really very merciful.

Like meekness, mercy is a distinctively Christian grace, little exhibited among non-Christians, and, alas, all too little among Christians too. Our fallen natures are geared more to criticism and retaliation than to mercy.

It is not only a compassionate feeling; it expresses itself in merciful activity. Pity must graduate from sterile emotion to compassionate action before it is mercy. We must stand in the shoes of the other person, think ourselves into their feelings, and then act accordingly.

The man of compassion does not condone wrong, but he is ready to put the best construction on ambiguous conduct. He will make every allowance rightly admissible for those who have failed, and will be alongside them to encourage them to start again.

Our personal experience may well be the rebound of our own attitude, for it is those who show mercy who receive mercy. The person who is reluctant to show to others the mercy of which he has been so lavish a recipient from God is in a perilous position (Matt. 18 : 23–35).

> *Though justice be thy plea, consider this,*
> *That in the course of justice, none of us*
> *Should see salvation: we do pray for mercy;*
> *And that same prayer doth teach us all to render*
> *The deeds of mercy.*
>
> Shakespeare, *The Merchant of Venice*

Pure in Heart

Blessed are the *pure in heart* for they shall see God (v. 8).

The beatific vision is vouchsafed only to the pure in heart, for 'without holiness no man shall see the Lord'. The revelation of God is not granted to the mighty in intellect, unless it is accompanied by purity of heart.

The vision of God is not a matter of optics but of moral and spiritual affinity with Him. Cleanness of heart brings clearness of vision. Sin so befogs the heart, that God becomes invisible. There are moral conditions for spiritual vision.

Behind the word 'pure' lies the idea of 'freedom from alloy, unadulterated'. Sincerity and integrity, as opposed to what is false and insincere. Pure gold has no alloy, pure linen no spots.

Throughout the Sermon, Jesus consistently bypasses the external, cultic purity of the Pharisees, and insists on inward purity. He exposed their hypocrisy in this regard with scathing words: 'Now do ye Pharisees make clean the outside of the cup and platter; but your inward part is full of ravening and wickedness. Ye fools, did not he that made that which is without make that which is within also?' (Luke 11:39).

Many would seek deliverance from morally impure thoughts and habits, who do not desire God's holiness in every other area of their lives. For such, Bishop Gore has these wise words:

> A great many people are distressed by impure temptations, and they fail to make progress with them for one reason, namely, that while they are anxious to get rid of sin in this one respect, they are not trying after righteousness as a whole. Uncleanness of heart and life they dislike. It weighs upon their conscience and destroys their self-respect. But they have no similar horror of pride or irreverence or uncharity . . .
>
> The way to get over uncleanness is, in innumerable cases, not to fight against that only, but to contend for positive holiness all round; for Christlikeness, for purity of heart in the sense in which Christ used the expression . . . is a will set straight towards God . . .
>
> There is an old Latin proverb, 'Unless the vessel is clean, whatever you pour into it turns sour.' It is so with the human will. Unless the will is directed straight for God, whatever you pour into the life, of religious and moral effort has a root of bitterness and sourness in it which spoils the whole life.[2]

'*You held not to whatsoever was true,*'
   Said my own voice talking to me.
'*Whatsoever was just you were slack to see,*
   Kept not things lovely and pure in view,'
   Said my own voice talking to me.

Thomas Hardy

But with Christ as the fountain of all purity dwelling in our hearts and communicating His own purity to us through the Holy Spirit, the maintenance of a pure heart is no longer an impossibility, and the vision of God not a tantalising mirage.

Conciliatory in Ministry

Blessed are the *peace-makers*, for they shall be called the children of God (v. 9).

Our Lord here asserts that the superlatively happy are those who create harmony, who reconcile people who are estranged, in whose healing presence tension and discord give way to harmony and peace. 'O the bliss of the conciliator!'

This beatitude is very frequently misread, and its true significance missed. It is not, 'Blessed are the *peace-lovers*', the placid, the pacifists. For the citizen of the kingdom of righteousness there can be no such thing as peaceful co-existence with evil. There is such a thing as a false peace which Christ came to destroy.

Nor is it a peace procured by *evasion of issues*, peace at any price. The peace-maker is prepared to pay the cost of his conciliation—and there is usually a heavy price to pay—but he will not compromise on principle.

Nor is the beatitude for *peace-keepers*, keepers of a peace already in existence. There is a world of difference between passively keeping peace and actively making peace. Jesus has in view not a passive virtue but a sacrificial activity.

The *peace-maker* achieves conciliation by allowing his own peace to be broken, and for this there is a notable precedent. 'He made peace by the blood of His cross', and for us a cross will be involved too. It is a ministry which calls for uncommon tact, insight, courage and patience, blended with warm love, but it pays high dividends.

'They shall be called sons of God.' This has reference to reputation, not to pedigree. They will be known by their likeness to their heavenly Father.

Here is something to covet, a reputation not only for being a lover of peace, but a healer of breaches, a promoter of unity, one who pours oil on troubled water.

> *Lord, make me an instrument of thy peace;*
> *That where there is hatred, I may bring love;*
> *That where there is wrong I may bring forgiveness;*
> *That where there is discord I may bring harmony;*
> *That where there is error I may bring truth;*
> *That where there is doubt I may bring faith;*
> *That where there is despair I may bring hope;*
> *That where there are shadows I may bring light;*
> *That where there is sadness, I may bring joy.*
>
> Francis of Assisi

Unwavering in Loyalty

> Blessed are they that are *persecuted* for righteousness' sake : for theirs is the Kingdom of heaven. Blessed are ye when men shall revile you and persecute you, and shall say all manner of evil against you falsely, for My sake. Rejoice and be exceeding glad, for great is your reward in heaven : for so persecuted they the prophets which were before you (vv. 10–12).

Even the peace-maker is not exempt from reviling and persecution, as the experience of the Master demonstrates. In our work for Christ and the Kingdom we may suffer insult or even injury, but even this can carry its freight of bliss.

There is, of course, no bliss in the reviling or persecution itself, but in the compensations it brings, or the fruit it bears. Joy in suffering is peculiar to Christianity, and reveals its supernatural origin.

But how can persecution be profitable or pain pleasant? For Paul said, 'I can even enjoy weakness . . .' A clue is given in the tense of the verb. It is not, 'Blessed are they that *are* persecuted,' but 'Blessed are they that *have been* persecuted'. The bliss is the outcome of a persecution and reviling that is past!

Early Christians would draw great comfort from this beatitude, for persecution was to them an all-too-common experience. This thought imported an entirely new dimension into their sufferings. The path of their discipleship was often a tortured one. For Christ's sake they were liable to lose their work and have their social and family life disrupted. Often it involved division in the home when some members were not Christians, and the political issue of loyalty to Caesar impaled them on the horns of an agonising dilemma. It must have brought great comfort and fresh courage to them to have this divine assurance of the bliss of the persecuted.

Jesus made it clear, however, that not all persecution or reviling brings blessing, by stipulating three qualifying conditions for this bliss:

It must be 'for righteousness' sake' (v. 10)—because he will do right, whatever the cost to himself. Sometimes Christians bring reviling or persecution upon themselves because of their tactlessness or angularity or inconsistency of walk. There is an unctuous piety that draws unnecessary opprobrium on the cause of Christ. There can be an aggressiveness in witnessing for Christ that does not commend the Gospel, and stirs up unnecessary antagonism.

The reviling must be falsely based (v. 11). There must be no just cause for the reproach in the life and

35

testimony of the disciple. He has not brought it on himself through his own sin or failure.

It must be for Christ's sake (v. 12)—arising out of the disciple's unwavering loyalty to his Master and King. Ill treatment which stems from our love to Christ and wise zeal for the extension of His Kingdom on earth will bring its own magnificent reward. 'Great is your reward in heaven.'

The Master deeply appreciates our willingness to 'go forth unto him without the camp, bearing his reproach (Heb. 13:13), and to enter into the 'fellowship of His sufferings'. The compensation is His special nearness and companionship in the experience. The three young men who were cast into Nebuchadnezzar's furnace discovered to their joy that in the midst of the seven times heated fires of persecution, the Son of God bore them company, and caused the flames to burn with a strange discrimination.

To our Lord's Jewish audience this must have been a startlingly new conception of persecution, for they had been taught to view it as a curse from God. To be told that persecution was the source of joy and bliss was revolutionary teaching indeed.

All these attractive qualities were exhibited by the Lord during His life on earth. But when a hostile world saw the Sermon on the Mount lived out perfectly before their very eyes, exemplified in terms of human life, they consigned Him to a cross.

The servant is not greater than his Lord. For Him, the incentive for endurance was 'the joy that was set before him'. For the disciple there is the incentive of promised bliss here and now and the prospect of great reward in heaven.

1. A. W. Tozer, *The Pursuit of God* (London, Oliphants, 1969), p. 109.

2. Charles Gore, *The Sermon on the Mount* (London, Hodder and Stoughton), p. 40.

4

The Savour of the Disciple's Witness

Matthew 5 : 13–16

> Ye are the salt of the earth. Ye are the light of the world.

In the Beatitudes, Jesus presented the ideal of Christian character, and indicated the compensations such a character brings. He now proceeds to define the role of the Christian in the world, for character expresses itself in conduct. Christian character is manifested in Christian influence, which Jesus likens to salt, light, and a city set on a hill.

Salt and Light

The disciple is salt amid earth's corruption and light in the midst of the world's darkness. It is to be noted that Jesus did not tell His followers that they were to be salt, or carry salt, or scatter salt. He said, 'Ye *are* salt', 'Ye *are* light', for He was not speaking of an activity but an influence. Though often unseen and unnoticed, the Christian exercises a potent influence in society.

In these two figures of speech there is both comparison and contrast. As to *comparison*, each stresses the *distinctiveness* of the disciple. He is known by his unlikeness to the people around him. Not that he

37

withdraws from society, but there is about him a spiritual separation, an atmosphere of the Holy Spirit so different from the spirit of the world that it makes him a marked man. The citizen of the Kingdom differs from most men of the world in both standards and practice.

Both salt and light *make their presence felt*. The absence or presence of either is immediately noticed. Each has its own distinctive contribution to make to society. The disciple is no negative factor in the world. His internal worth and his external witness each makes its impression on the people among whom he moves.

Both salt and light are absolutely *indispensable* to normal living. Life is not normal to an invalid who is on an insipid, salt-free diet. Life is not normal to a person who like Christiana Tsai, the Queen of the Dark Chamber, has to spend her life in heavily subdued light. Without salt, food is tasteless. Without light, life is gloomy and depressing. 'Salt stands for pervading influence, light for revealing radiance.' As Pliny the Younger[1] said, 'Nothing is more useful than salt and sunshine', and the true disciple exhibits the distinctive features of both.

But there are equally clear *contrasts*. The function of salt is negative. It prevents deterioration and corruption. Our Lord's fishermen disciples would readily understand this figure from their accustomed salting down of the fish they sent to Jerusalem for sale. The function of light is positive. It fills the house with brightness. The disciple fulfils a negative preservative function in society by the quality of his character, but he also sheds a radiance about him by his active promotion of all that is pure and good.

Again, salt acts secretly while light shines publicly. The function of salt is essentially a hidden one. Unobserved it carries on its aseptic activity, but light can never be hidden. Publicity is the essence of its contribution.

> Ye are the salt of the earth, but if the salt have lost its savour, wherewith shall it be salted? It is thenceforth good for nothing, but to be cast out and trodden underfoot of men (v. 13).

Salt is the foe of insipidity. The disciple walking in close fellowship with his Master will not be pale and insipid in personality. By daily company with Christ and drawing on His graces he must inevitably absorb and display in increasing measure his Lord's distinctiveness. His speech, for example, though 'always with grace, seasoned with salt'—will not be insipid, but pungent, and aseptic. He will have the moral influence, and if necessary the moral courage to check unsavoury or critical talk. His own conversation will be constructive. There will be a 'tang' about him that evidences the difference Christ makes in a life.

It was said of Lord Cairns that whenever he entered the British Parliament, no matter how late the hour or how acrid the atmosphere had been, his presence always brought peace and harmony. And the secret? No matter what hour he arrived home he made a practice of spending two hours in prayer and devotion the next morning before commencing his day's work. That accounted for the fact that to an amazing degree he was salt in the sordid world of politics.

Salt is also the foe of corruption. It destroys germs and fights harmful bacteria. It imparts its own wholesomeness to whatever it touches. Just as salt combats and arrests physical decay, so the disciple who is in vital touch with his Master combats and arrests corruption in society to a degree that is not always immediately visible. Without the hidden salt of Christian influence, civilisation would have crumbled long ago.

In His employment of this figure Jesus tacitly condemned a false conception of separation from the world.

Salt can fulfil its function only as it makes vital contact with the food it is to season or preserve. The disciple must have meaningful contact with the non-Christian people whom he is to influence. In a recent letter from a friend these percipient words occurred: 'The place of the salt is not in the salt-shaker, but in the soup—and the world is the soup!' Salt will never exercise its seasoning or preservative power if the salt remains on one plate and the meat on the other.

It is to be feared that evangelical Christianity has been characterised too much by the salt-shaker mentality. Separation from the world has been presented as *isolation* from the world, rather than as *insulation* from the world. This was not the attitude of the Master. One of the charges hurled at Him by the scrupulous Pharisees was, 'This man receiveth sinners and eateth with them'. And yet was He not 'separate from sinners'? Clearly His separation was not of the body but of the spirit.

Living a life ensphered in the Holy Spirit as He did, He was insulated from the evil around Him, while yet moving with the greatest naturalness, in closest contact with sinful men.

The Salvation Army lassie entering hotels and saloon bars to sell her *War Cry* with its message of salvation, is 'separate from sinners' and kept safe by the Holy Spirit, although elbow by elbow with them.

There is no place in our Lord's teaching for hermit Christianity. We can influence people for Christ only as we earn the right to do so by knowing and loving and serving them.

This metaphor of salt poses some very searching questions for self-examination. Am I aseptic in my influence or do I spread the virus of sin? Is my life pungent or insipid? Do I live an insulated or an isolated life? Has the type of separation I have practised cut me off from fruitful contact with people of the world such as those among whom the Lord moved so freely?

It is a sobering thought that salt can lose its savour. The glistening whiteness may still be present, but the astringent flavour missing. The salt of Palestine was not pure, but adulterated with other minerals. When exposed to rain or sun it tended to lose its distinctive savour and ability to arrest corruption. It then became *good for nothing*—ominous words.

So can the disciple lose his distinctive influence for Christ in the world. He loses his savour when he allows the impurities and standards of the world to infiltrate his spiritual life. He becomes powerless to arrest the drift into the morass of corruption of those around him. Since vital Christianity is the only salt of the earth, when the disciple loses that, what can take its place? Good for nothing!

LIGHT—THE RADIANCE OF THE DISCIPLE

Ye are the light of the world (v. 14).

If salt represents secret influence, then light stands for luminous radiance. If salt is unconscious influence, light is conscious influence. If salt signifies internal worth, light stands for external witness.

God had selected Israel to be 'a light to the nations' (Isa. 49:6), but in this they grievously disappointed Him. Jesus now delegates this responsibility to the disciples He has chosen. They had kindled their torches at the Light of the world, and now they in turn are to be light to the nations of the world. And so, early in His ministry, in these pregnant words, the Lord of the harvest issued His Galilean call to world-wide witness. Their sphere of witness was to be nothing less than 'the world'.

But theirs was only a borrowed light. He was the Light, they were luminaries (Phil. 2:15). He was the Sun, collectively they were the moon, reflecting the Sun's light.

He who said to them. 'Ye are the light of the world', also said, 'I am the light of the world.' Only by constant contact with the Light could they fulfil their role of luminaries in a dark world.

Jesus told His disciples that they were 'the light', not *the lights* of the world. He was thus indicating that it was as a group, the Church, that they are the light of the world—not as individuals. His Kingdom can do without rugged individualism. His disciples are fellow servants and fellow workers, following the directions of the same Master, not following their own plans and programmes.

Many Christian workers fail to master this fundamental truth, with resulting fragmentation, and not infrequently spiritual disaster to themselves and others. Each must have his own little light, must run his own little show, largely because he is not humble enough and not spiritual enough to obey the command, 'Submit yourselves one to another in the fear of God.' The result is a great deal of abortive though well-intentioned effort, and a great waste of the Lord's money. This is, of course, a generalisation to which there are glorious exceptions, and when there is sincerity of motive the Lord often overrules human failure. But the principle remains true.

Light is to illuminate, and dispel the surrounding darkness. Our Christianity should be clearly visible to the world, not confined to the four walls of the church. Failure in this respect is one of the main reasons for the minimal impact our churches usually make in the godless communities in which they are located.

Light is to guide in the darkness. Guided by beacon lights, ships .traverse safely the sea lanes of the world by night as well as by day. Such is our beneficent and responsible ministry. The light of our testimony can serve to guide others through the rocks and reefs of the sea of life.

Light is to warn of the dangers of the darkness. By the

unwavering light of his Christian witness, many a man has saved another from shipwreck.

Light is to be diffused, and not concealed. Jesus underlined this in the figures of the bushel measure and the bed. In those days there were no matches to kindle a fire, so it was customary to preserve some embers for this purpose. For safety, they would often be kept under an earthen bushel measure, and this custom may have given rise to the Lord's illustration. Light is not to be placed under a bushel or a bed, or it will be unable to fulfil its function.

> Neither do men light a candle and put it under a bushel, but on a candlestick and it giveth light unto all that are in the house (v. 15).

The light is set on a stand, in a conspicuous place, not that it may be seen, but that it might shed its radiance throughout the whole house. Is it not true that the witness of many a disciple has been quenched by being hidden under the bushel of business or the bed of laziness? (Mark 4: 21).

A CITY SET ON A HILL—THE PROMINENCE OF THE DISCIPLE

> A city that is set on a hill cannot be hid (v. 14).

It may be that as Jesus spoke, He pointed out some city on a nearby mountain. A city is an aggregation of houses. Jesus is not speaking here of an isolated house, but of a community. Christianity knows nothing of solitary religion. The lighted house is multiplied until it becomes an illuminated city that cannot be concealed —a growth which is symbolic of the irresistible, ongoing witness of the ideal New Testament church.

Christians are set on the skyline. Like their Master they cannot be hid. The Church is to be a landmark in a spiritual as well as a physical sense. 'Eminent piety is evident piety.'

43

Like John the Baptist, the church at Antioch was 'a burning and a shining light' in the darkness of contemporary heathenism. So luminous was its witness, that at the peak of its spiritual power, it was said that of every two citizens of Antioch, one was a Christian. Small wonder that it was this church our Lord chose to launch His world missionary enterprise.

The words of our Lord in verse 16 summarise the lessons of this paragraph:

> Let your light so shine before men, that they may see your good works, and glorify your Father which is in heaven.

There is no objection to our good works being noticed. Indeed, they ought to be noticed by men in order that God may be glorified in them. But that must never be the inspiring motive. 'Men are not to see the lamp, but the shining, and to give God the praise.'

1. See Plummer, *Exegetical Commentary on Matthew*, p. 71.

5

The Sacredness of the Divine Revelation

Matthew 5 : 17–20

The Preacher has delineated the character and indicated the role of the ideal citizen of His Kingdom. He now anticipates and proceeds to answer a question which would inevitably arise in the minds of the more thoughtful of His hearers.

ATTITUDE TO PRIOR REVELATION

The teaching He had already given was so paradoxical, so radical, even revolutionary in its challenge to the current teaching of the nation's religious leaders, that it would not be surprising if they were tempted to think Him just another irresponsible incendiary, bent on overthrowing the Establishment. In a nation, and at a time when new revolutionaries appeared on the scene with monotonous regularity, this wandering preacher may be yet another. Jesus therefore felt it necessary to clarify His relation to the existing religious order and to Old Testament revelation. This He proceeds to do.

Think not that I am come to destroy the law, or the prophets: I am not come to destroy but to fulfil. For verily I say unto you, Till heaven and earth pass away, one jot or one tittle shall in no wise pass from the law till all be fulfilled. Whosoever therefore shall break one of these least commandments, and shall teach men so, he shall be called the least in the kingdom of heaven: but whosoever shall do and teach them, the same shall be called great in the kingdom of heaven (v. 17–19).

By this unequivocal statement, the Lord achieved a dual purpose. On the one hand He dispelled the suspicion of the devout Jews of the right wing, whose conservatism and reverence for the Law made them suspicious of any change or innovation. There are such in every religious community and organisation. On the other hand, He at the same time defused the inflammatory hopes and expectations of the radicals of the left wing, who were always itching for insurrection.

In this way He assured His hearers that His Kingdom was not in any sense out of harmony with Old Testament revelation *correctly interpreted*. But He soon demonstrated that He was utterly out of sympathy with the traditional and externalised interpretations of the scribes and Pharisees. It was at this point that His battle with the religious leaders was joined in earnest.

Jesus was no revolutionary iconoclast. His mission was constructive, not destructive. He had not come to scrap or invalidate the Law which He held in reverence as the very word of His Father. He neither renounced nor denounced it, but exalted it and made it honourable. His reinterpretation of it indicated that the moral demands of His new order were even more stringent and searching than those of the Pharisees. He deepened the significance of the Law's requirements, and intensified its meaning and application.

Nor was He a careless antinomian. He did not relax

the requirements of the Law, or release men from its moral and spiritual obligations. True, His disciples are no longer 'under the law' as a way of salvation or means of justification (Rom. 3:20; Gal. 3:11, 13). But 'the righteousness of the law' is still to be fulfilled in them (Rom. 8:4), and they will always be 'under law to Christ' (1 Cor. 9:21). But this makes all the difference. As Bishop Moule put it, 'Your dealings as debtors are now not with the enemy who cried for your death, but with the Friend who has bought you out of his power.' The former relationship of law has now become one of love.

During World War II there was a man who lived in an Australian mining town who dressed in sombre black on Sundays and carried a very large black Bible to church. He was referred to as 'the biggest Bible-basher' in the town. He was equally notorious as the biggest black-marketeer in the town! When approached by a young preacher who felt impelled to face him with the adverse effects of his bad testimony in the community, he replied with complete aplomb: 'But I am not under law, I am under grace!'

The relation of grace to law has often been misinterpreted in this way, and 'grace' has been used as a cloak for unethical conduct. But those who adopt this trick of interpretation overlook the fact that of the Ten Commandments, nine are reiterated in the New Testament. Their moral obligations are therefore still binding on all Christians (see Mark 10:19–22; Rom. 7:7; 13:8–10; Col. 3:9; James 2:8–13; 5:12; 1 John 5:21). Significantly, the lone commandment which is not reiterated in the New Testament is the fourth which relates to sabbath observance—an unfortunate omission for Seventh-day Adventists.

Fulfilling the Law
The word 'destroy' used by Jesus in v. 17 carries the meaning, 'to loosen down', as of a tent; 'to invalidate'.

'Fulfil' means 'to fill full', as in Matt. 23:32. Jesus came to complete and fill out the Law, and to reveal the full depth of meaning it was intended to hold.

In this sense Jesus fulfilled the ceremonial aspects of the Law which pointed to Him, as well as the moral law which He scrupulously observed. His teaching in the Sermon makes clear that while its ceremonial aspects were no longer necessary—they had found their perfect fulfilment in Him—the moral and spiritual principles it enshrines are imperishable and of continuing validity.

In what sense, then, did Jesus come to fulfil the Law?

Negatively, not as it was being interpreted and enforced by the fastidious but hypocritical Pharisees. They had so encrusted the Law with their traditions as to almost nullify it.

They externalised it, reducing it to a legal code covering every conceivable situation, with thousands of pettifogging rules and regulations. In their eyes, for example, it was a breach of the Law to write or to heal someone on the sabbath. From this false and trifling interpretation, Jesus came to set men free. By interpreting the true spiritual meaning of the Law, He released them from the legalistic bondage under which they had so long been oppressed, without lowering the standard. The remainder of the chapter is occupied with this re-interpretation of the Law.

Positively, Jesus came to fulfil the Law in a fourfold sense.

He fulfilled it *historically* by becoming man, 'born of a woman, born under the law' (Gal. 4:4). Only in this way could the types and prophecies of the Old Testament be fulfilled. In His death on the cross, no fewer than thirty-three prophecies found their fulfilment. In his Gospel, Matthew gives special prominence to this aspect of truth in the oft-repeated formula, 'that the Scripture might be fulfilled'.

48

Even in the hour of death Jesus was concerned that no prophecy concerning Him as the promised Messiah should remain unfulfilled. Throughout the whole ordeal no expression of the physical agony He was enduring had escaped His lips. It took the prophetic expression of His Father's will to unseal His lips: 'That the Scripture might be fulfilled, he saith, I thirst!'

He fulfilled the Law *vicariously* in His perfect life on earth. Israel, and indeed all men, had failed to render to God the perfect obedience to His commands which the Law required, so Jesus stepped into the breach. As the theologians state it, 'He satisfied the demands of the Law by His active and passive obedience', with the happy result that His disciples are 'redeemed from the curse of the law'. He incorporated and worked out its principles in His own life and ministry—for us men who had so conspicuously failed. He was thus qualified to stand in our place.

He fulfilled the Law *sacrificially*. His one and perfect atoning sacrifice satisfied its last demand, for He assumed all the liabilities to the Law standing to our account, and discharged them. In His death, He exhausted the sanctions of the Law in His own blood, and paid the penalty for our breach of it.

And may we not say that He fulfilled the Law *exegetically*, by giving its true inner meaning, by revealing its deep spiritual application? By repudiating the traditional accretions of the Pharisees, Jesus opened the way for His disciples to appreciate its beauty and significance. He promulgated an ethic of love which is the fulfilling of the Law (Rom. 13 : 10).

His statement also confirmed the harmony, unity and continuity of the old order and the new order He had come to initiate. Since both had come from the same Source, they were all of one piece. The Old Testament is the gospel in bud, the New the gospel in flower. Though not imperfect, the old revelation was incomplete, and Jesus came to complete it.

Christ's attitude to the Old Testament Scriptures is a matter of great importance to His followers in every age. If He held them loosely, then so may they. If He treated them with full and reverent acceptance, then so must they.

How did He regard them? His attitude was made unequivocally plain in the words, 'Verily I say unto you, till heaven and earth pass, one jot or one tittle shall in no wise pass from the Law till all be fulfilled' (v. 18).

On their face value these words appear to teach that the smallest detail of the Law will last till the end of time, and the words that follow indicate that the place of the disciple in the Kingdom will be determined by his attitude to that Law. But this interpretation is not acceptable to many modern scholars, who maintain that these words were not those of Jesus, but that Matthew put them into His mouth.

This viewpoint is expressed in A. M. Hunter's usually helpful exposition, *Design for Life*, where he writes:

> These verses as they stand can hardly be the words of Christ: for (a) the doctrine of the Law's permanence is pure rabbinism; and (b) Jesus Himself relaxed the sabbath law, annulled the law about purity, and rejected Moses' command about divorce. They read rather like some early Jewish misapplication of some words of Jesus . . . what we have in Matthew is Christian legalism such as may have arisen in ultra-conservative circles which were shocked by the attitude of Paul and his friends to the Law.[1]

But is this not rather a cavalier way to treat the text of Scripture because a passage presents some problems of interpretation? Jesus prefaced this statement with the distinctive formula He used when making some utterance of unusual importance: 'Verily I say unto you . . .' To determine which are and which are not the genuine sayings of Jesus by such arbitrary and subjective means, is not acceptable to the evangelical Christian who accepts the full inspiration and authority of the canonical Scriptures. Are other sayings of Jesus which commence with the same formula also to be dispensed with at the whim of the exegete?

This passage, along with many others, leaves the unmistakable impression that our Lord entertained a very high view of the inspiration of the Old Testament Scriptures. Even after His resurrection, when all human limitations had been laid aside, there was no diminution of His reverence for the Law and the Prophets, or any rectification of the attitude He had adopted during His earthly life.

The expression, 'till heaven and earth pass away', probably means 'till the present cosmic system ceases to exist'. That Jesus does not here speak of absolute perpetuity can be deduced from the fact that He elsewhere indicated that it *would* cease to exist. 'Heaven and earth shall pass away, but my words shall not pass away' (Matt 24:35).

Our equivalent of 'jot' and 'tittle' would be the dot of an 'i' and the stroke of a 't'. Our Lord's apparent meaning is that not the minutest element of the spirit and teaching of the Scriptures would be abrogated so long as time lasts. 'Fulfilled' in v. 18 is a different word from that in v. 17, and conveys the meaning, 'till the whole purpose is accomplished'.

In v. 19 Jesus warns His hearers of the danger of disannulling even the least of God's commandments, either in doctrine or in practice. 'Break' here refers not so much to the practical transgression of an acknowledged law, as to teaching that certain portions of Scripture are not to be regarded as valid. Dean Alford affirms that Christ's words are decisive against such persons, whether ancient or modern, as would set aside the Old

Testament as without significance, or as inconsistent with the New.

History and experience unite to prove that not infrequently the one who teaches in public that any command of God is not important, is himself breaking it in private. Having outraged his own conscience, he endeavours to quieten it by teaching that it is not so important after all.

Christ's test of greatness given in this verse, is another of His striking reversals of values that will come to light in the day of final appraisal. 'Whosoever shall do and teach them—these least commandments—shall be called great in the Kingdom of heaven.' The one who deflects from God's standard and teaches others similarly to treat it lightly, lowers his status in the Kingdom.

> The Master stood upon the mount, and taught.
>   He saw a fire in His disciples' eyes.
> 'The old Law,' they said, 'is wholly come to nought;
>   Behold the new world rise'.
>
> 'Was it,' the Lord then said, 'with scorn ye saw
>   The old Law observed by scribes and Pharisees?
> I say unto you, see that ye keep that Law
>   More faithfully than these.'
>
> 'Too hasty heads for ordering words, alas,
>   Think not that I to annul the Law have willed.
> No jot, no tittle from the Law shall pass,
>   Till all shall be fulfilled.'
>
>   Matthew Arnold

Superior Righteousness

Jesus made yet another daring and revolutionary statement which must have bewildered His disciples, and certainly would not improve His standing with the religious leaders.

For I say unto you, That except your righteousness shall exceed the righteousness of the Scribes and Pharisees, ye shall in no case enter into the kingdom of heaven (v. 20).

That is, they must be better than the most religious people of their day! In what sense must their righteousness exceed that of the Pharisees? Not in quantity or in punctiliousness. The over-scrupulous Pharisees had reduced their righteousness to an outward and unspiritual conformity to the Mosaic code, which entirely bypassed its spirit. There was no heart and sincerity in it. Exact observance of ceremonies was the most important thing, not love to God and showing mercy to man. Their whole religious life had become artificial and superficial.

Jesus emphasised the necessity of genuineness and reality—no less necessary now than then. He demanded of His disciples then—as now—a higher, more spiritual expression in fervent, sacrificial love to God and man; for the essence of the Law is not keeping rules, but showing mercy, not legislation, but love.

Having now cleared the ground of false and mistaken ideas concerning the Law, Jesus asserted His right as Supreme Legislator to supersede it, even as the complete supersedes the incomplete. He widens and deepens its application. An author has the right to do what he wills with his own writings, for he alone knows their inner significance.

Five times Jesus quoted the Law in the remainder of chapter 5. In each case He contradicted the interpretation of the Pharisees and substituted His own interpretation. Consulting no one, He had the audacity 'to correct the most sacred writings out of His own wisdom'. Six times the audacious formula is employed: 'Ye have heard that it was said . . . But I say unto you . . .'

In saying this, He was not faulting the Law of Moses, but was correcting the traditional interpretation and apprehension of it. By saying, 'Ye have heard', and not, 'It is written', Jesus shrewdly distinguished the actual text from the Pharisees' commentary on it.

1. A. M. Hunter, *Design for Life* (London, S.C.M., 1953), p. 43.

6

The Spirituality of the
Disciple's Attitudes

Matthew 5 : 21–48

In the remainder of chapter 5 Jesus presents five examples of the way in which the traditions and superficial interpretations of the Pharisees had emasculated the teachings of the Law and Prophets.

In each case He re-interprets them, correcting the fallacies and at the same time laying bare the underlying spiritual principles. As illustrations He uses murder, adultery, false swearing, revenge and malice. From the depths of the devilish impulse to kill a fellow man, Jesus leads His hearers up to the sublime heights of love, even for an enemy.

SELF-CONTROL VERSUS FORBIDDEN ANGER

> Ye have heard that it was said by them of old time, Thou shalt not kill; and whosoever shall kill shall be in danger of the judgment: But I say unto you, That whosoever is angry with his brother (without cause) shall be in danger of the judgment: and whosoever shall say to his brother, Raca, shall be in danger of the council: but whosoever shall say, Thou fool, shall be in danger of hell fire (vv. 21–2).

This first example of the new standards of the Kingdom highlights our Lord's estimation of the sacredness of life and personality.

In His exposition and expansion of the sixth commandment, 'Thou shalt not kill', Jesus asserts that murder goes deeper than the overt act. A story is told of the great American preacher, Henry Ward Beecher, who was having constant trouble with the clock in his church. It was always either too fast or too slow. One day, in exasperation, he put a sign over it which read, 'Don't blame my hands, the trouble lies deeper.'

Murder is a crime, not of the hand but of the heart; in the motive, not in the act alone. In this revolutionary statement Jesus puts anger, whether nursed secretly in the heart, or expressed in passionate or contemptuous speech, in the same category as murder. Both have a killing tendency. A man's soul can be murdered as effectively by contemptuous and angry speech as his body by a knife. Can the widespread racial strife abroad in the world today not be traced in part to this evil source?

There is general agreement that the words 'without a cause', should be omitted from verse 22. The phrase does not appear in any of the more important manuscripts and is omitted in most of the later translations. This means that whether with, or without, provocation anger is absolutely forbidden.

It is significant that of two Greek words for anger, one meaning anger that quickly flares up but soon dies down, and the other anger that broods and becomes deep-seated, it is the latter which Jesus here employs.

Anger and contempt are the seed-plot of murder. A heart filled with rage, resentment and contempt is a murderous heart. The Pharisees were not concerned with sin until it blossomed into action. They considered they had observed the sixth commandment if they refrained from actual homicide. The state of heart of the offender was no concern of theirs.

But Jesus denounced all anger, all passionate and contemptuous speech and extended the conception of murder to the motivating thought or words which preceded it. By-passing the act of murder, He raised the whole standard of guilt, by tracing it back to the evil motive. He also showed that there are degrees of sin and corresponding degrees of retribution.

1. *Malicious anger* nursed in the heart, which brings the offender in danger of 'the judgment'. This phrase does not refer primarily to future judgment, although that is involved too, but to the judgment of the local council, the inferior court in each town which was empowered to deal with the less serious offences.

2. *Contemptuous speech*, the outcropping of the arrogant contempt that despises another. '*Raca*' is a term of contempt, anger expressed in insulting words such as, 'You blockhead! You simpleton!' It is the intellectual snobbery that despises lesser breeds. Those who harbour such a spirit and express it in this way, Jesus said, are in danger of the more severe judgment of the Sanhedrin, the Supreme Court of the Jews.

3. *Uncontrolled rage* exploding into passionate speech : 'You scoundrel : You cursed fool!' These are aspersions cast, not on the mental ability of the victim, but on his moral character. The word 'fool' in this connection is an insult and has reference to a man's morals. He who thus robs a man of his moral character is in danger of 'the Gehenna of fire'.

This is generally accepted as a reference to the Valley of Hinnom outside Jerusalem, a place where, in former days some Jews had sacrificed their children to the loathsome god Moloch. It was the place where the refuse of the city was consumed in fires which were always burning. It was the place where the bodies of the worst criminals were cast. To the Jews there could be no more terrible figure of reprobation and retribution. The term is used elsewhere for the place of punishment after death. It is a terrible thing to filch a man's reputation, and it brings its own retribution.

> Good name in man or woman, dear my lord,
> Is immediate jewel of their souls:
> Who steals my purse steals trash; 'tis something,
>   nothing:
> 'Twas mine, 'tis his, and has been slave to thousands;
> But he that filches from me my good name
> Robs me of that which not enriches him
> And makes me poor indeed.
>
> Shakespeare, *Othello*

Uncontrolled anger brings on itself an automatic retribution. Discoveries in the realm of psychiatry reveal that passion, resentment, jealousy, desire for revenge and similar emotions produce poisonous secretions in the body that seriously affect health. So anger has a murderous tendency towards the one who acts as host to it.

The question naturally arises, 'Is it never right to be angry?' The fact that Scripture contains the injunction, 'Be ye angry and sin not; let not the sun go down on your wrath' (Eph. 4:26), is an indication that there is a permissible anger. But even then it must be controlled, and not allowed to continue, lest it degenerate into sin, and an unforgiving spirit. We are not to go to bed angry.

As to the nature of this permissible anger, a study of the occasions on which Jesus Himself was angry will afford us light. Two such occasions are recorded. The first, Mark 3:5, was not the expression of personal temper and rancour, but of anger accompanied by grief at the hardness of the hearts of the religious leaders. He was angry at their callousness in the presence of human suffering.

In the second instance, His anger was a holy jealousy for His Father's interests, and indignation at the manner in which mercenary priests and merchants had desecrated His Father's house. They had turned

58

the house of prayer into a sordid trading post (John 2:15–17).

The important point to note is that Jesus was never angry at the way men maltreated and insulted Him, only at their attitude to His Father and their fellow men. His anger was entirely free from self-interest, and this is the test of sinless anger. Anger becomes sinful when it terminates on self. When tempted to anger, let us make doubly sure that ours is not sinful anger.

Restitution and Reconciliation

> Therefore if thou bring thy gift to the altar and there rememberest that thy brother hath ought against thee, leave there thy gift before the altar, and go thy way; first be reconciled to thy brother, and then come and offer they gift (vv. 23–4).

The connection with the previous paragraph is not difficult to see. If we have sinned against our brother in any of the ways mentioned above—or in any other way—and in the place of prayer the Holy Spirit brings to remembrance the fact that he has a valid accusation against us, our first responsibility is not to continue the ritual of worship, but to effect the restoration of ruptured fellowship.

'*First go . . . then come and offer thy gift*' is the invariable order. We are to hold up our worship until our relationship with our brother is one of Christian love. God is more interested in correct relationships than in gifts. Reconciliation precedes sacrifice. It is impossible to be wrong with our brother, and right with God. Jesus says the initiative lies with us, not with the offended brother.

At one of the early Keswick Conventions in England in 1903 Dr F. B. Meyer delivered an address on this text which so moved the great audience to action in making restitution, that the post office at Keswick ran short of postal notes and money orders. A relevant portion of this address follows. After asserting that it was impossible to expect God to accept our gifts and to fill us with the Holy Spirit until things were put right, Dr Meyer said:

> First, go to your brother and tell him you have done wrong; and make restitution. Write out the cheque tonight and send it; add the interest. Write the letter of apology, and say, 'Excuse me, and forgive me.'
>
> Have you been angry? . . . When a man allows anger in his soul it makes him stiff and abrupt and cold. Then Christ says, 'Have you let anger make you say of someone, "Vain fellow!" or "Ungovernable fool!"?' Directly you judge another man in that way, you are judged and by an invisible Court the sentence is pronounced on you that you pronounced.
>
> If you call a man a vain fellow, heaven pronounces that you are vain. If you speak of a man as a fool, the heavenly Court pronounces you culpable of folly. And if you count a man as rubbish, you yourself are cast on God's rubbish heap—Gehenna—which is not for the future but for now. There are scores of men and women in this tent who are on God's rubbish heap now. He cannot use them because they are not just and right in their relations to others.[1]

Obedience to the injunction of these verses has brought great blessing to individuals and churches. During a conference of most of the Protestant pastors of South Vietnam who met with a group of forty Western missionaries at which the author was privileged to minister in 1966, the Spirit moved in great power. From the first meeting hearts were melted, and a deepening conviction of sin and failure was manifest.

After one evening meeting, the delegates continued

in prayer, and continued into the early morning. Many were convicted of specific sins and of wrong attitudes and relationships. Then conviction turned to mutual confession. Quietly one pastor would go to another, acknowledging his wrong and seeking forgiveness and reconciliation; missionary went to missionary, pastor to missionary and missionary to pastor. As the tears flowed, fellowship was restored and hearts were fused in fervent love. What a shout of victory there was as we met the next day. Eternity will reveal what this time of adjustment meant to the Church and the progress of the gospel in beleaguered South Vietnam.

> Agree with thine adversary quickly, while thou art in the way with him; lest at any time the adversary deliver thee to the judge, and the judge deliver thee to the officer, and thou be cast into prison. Verily I say unto thee, Thou shalt by no means come out thence until thou hast paid the uttermost farthing (vv. 25-6).

Continuing to speak to the offending brother, Jesus exhorts him to effect a speedy reconciliation. Though the passage seems strange to us, it would be readily understood by the disciples. It was by no means uncommon in those days for two litigants to travel together to court, as in the case Jesus envisaged. While still travelling, there was yet time to effect an amicable settlement. He urged that the dispute be settled at once, while there was opportunity and before the judge gave irrevocable judgment.

His point was that where only personal interests and not principles are involved, compromise is better than prison. In case of debt, if he was adjudged guilty, the debtor would be handed over to the court officer who had the power to imprison him until the debt was liquidated.

By analogy we learn that as it is wisdom to be

reconciled with our adversary quickly and before judgment is given, so it is wisdom to be reconciled to our wronged brother before the judgment of God fall on us for our sin.

MORAL PURITY VERSUS FORBIDDEN DESIRE

> Ye have heard that it was said by them of old time, Thou shalt not commit adultery: But I say unto you, That whosoever looketh on a woman to lust after her hath committed adultery with her already in his heart (vv. 27–8).

As the second example of the new and higher law of His Kingdom, Jesus selected the seventh commandment which deals with another fundamental impulse, sex. As the underlying principle of the sixth commandment is the sacredness of life and personality, so the seventh is based on reverence for womanhood and the sacredness of the marriage relationship.

Although it is not explicitly stated, in this context 'adultery' seems to have a wider application than its strict definition—'voluntary intercourse of a married person with one of the opposite sex other than his or her spouse'.

In support of this contention one commentator writes:

> We are not to suppose from the word used here, 'adultery', that our Lord means to restrict this breach of this commandment to married persons, or to criminal intercourse with such. The expressions 'Whosoever looketh . . .', and 'looketh on a woman . . .' seem clearly to extend the range of the commandment to all forms of impurity, and the counsels which follow—as they were most certainly intended for all, whether married or unmarried—seem to confirm this.[2]

In this permissive age when morals have tobogganed to an all-time low, and incitements to moral laxity assault eye and ear from all directions, we must rediscover and proclaim this lost standard. Jesus made no apology for dealing with the sordid aspects of life, nor need we. Did He speak the last word on this subject, or is the last word with the 'new morality'? He warned against

1. Desecrating the Spirit of Marriage—Lust

Our Lord's attitude to moral purity contrasted strongly with that of the Pharisees. They would condemn and punish a man for the outward act of adultery, but were unconcerned whether or not his heart was filled with lust. Jesus went back behind the external act and traced the virus of his sin to the secret lust that inspired it 'in his heart'. He made it clear that the seventh commandment is infringed as totally by lax indulgence of eye and thought as by the immoral act.

Jesus was not in any sense condemning a natural and normal relationship between the sexes, in which each enjoys the company of the other. Nor was He speaking of the normal and natural stirring of the God-given sexual impulse. The Bible teaches purity, not prudery. God made us male and female, and sexual desire is an integral part of our human nature.

The tense and context of the verb 'looketh' (v. 28) indicate, not the involuntary glance, but a purposeful and repeated looking; looking to excite longing; using the eyes to awaken lust. What Jesus is condemning is the looking at a woman as a possible object for the gratification of desire; as an object to exploit, not as a person to be respected and loved; the look which disregards the sacredness of a woman's person.

Bacteria breed where there is a hospitable culture bed, and Jesus says this is provided by a lustful heart. While temptation to illicit sexual indulgence is not in itself sin, it quickly develops into sin when welcomed and entertained. Given favourable circumstances, it will soon break out into action. Many who secretly harbour impure thoughts are restrained from the sinful act only by lack of opportunity or fear of consequences. They are too cowardly to act out their thoughts, but in God's sight they have already committed the sin in their hearts.

The prescription

Jesus was too skilful a Physician to diagnose the disease and then not prescribe a remedy. In the next two verses He prescribes what steps should be taken to combat the disease

> And if thy right eye offend thee, pluck it out, and cast it from thee; for it is profitable for thee that one of thy members should perish, and not that thy whole body be cast into hell. And if thy right hand offend thee, cut it off, and cast it from thee : for it is profitable for thee that one of thy members should perish, and not that thy whole body should be cast into hell (vv. 29–30).

Rigorous self-discipline is the price of moral purity, but the goal is abundantly worth the cost involved. Eye and hand are here viewed as accomplices in temptation. The eye can be the inlet and the hand the executor of temptation. Both have to be dealt with drastically, as Jesus's counsel, 'pluck it out', 'cut it off' makes clear.

It has already been pointed out that these words are not to be followed literally, for cutting off the right hand would still leave the left to execute the sinful act. The vivid imagery means that anything which makes it easier for us to fall into this sin must be ruthlessly excised. As Charles Darwin once said, 'Whatever makes any bad action familiar to the mind, renders the performance so much easier.'

In a world where temptation to sexual laxity is so ubiquitous, we must be severe with ourselves, exercising a rigid self-discipline, otherwise the spark of temptation will kindle the inflammable material in our hearts. One familiar war maxim was 'The price of safety is unceasing vigilance', and it has a spiritual as well as a military relevance.

Drastic action may at times be necessary. Joseph lost his position but preserved his purity by taking to his heels and fleeing from his temptress.

The disciple must settle for the fact that in the interests of purity, there may need to be restrictions in his life. He may not be able to go to every place, read every book, view every TV programme or do everything that the non-Christian or the carnal Christian may feel free to do. But better a limited life than a defiled and defeated life. The athlete willingly accepts great restrictions in his life-pattern for the sake of the coveted prize. The lizard says, 'Better my tail than my life!' Peter speaks about 'eyes full of adultery'. When the eye is impure the vision of God is obscured, and the whole life suffers as a consequence.

The tense of the verbs in 'pluck it out' and 'cut it off' conveys the idea of doing it at once and once for all. It is not to be a gradual process but a critical act. Impure passion is to be mortified, not little by little, but once for all by a decisive act of the will. The natural must be sacrificed in the interests of the spiritual. David was tempted and fell because he kept on looking. Joseph faced an even more severe temptation but overcame by plucking out his right eye and cutting off his right hand.

Positive steps can be taken in the battle for purity, and among them is Paul's counsel: 'Whatsoever things are true . . . honest . . . just . . . pure . . . If there be any virtue and if there be any praise, *think on these things*' (Phil. 4:8).

The mind can entertain only one thought at a time, and we choose what that thought is. When a mind is preoccupied with what is pure, the impure is unable to gain entrance.

Further, it is a well-established psychological fact that the sexual drive can be sublimated, and find a satisfying outlet in creative art or in self-forgetful service for God and our fellow men.

Finally, the look of lust can be defeated by the look of trust. Looking to Jesus, our omnipotent Lord, with confidence in His willingness and ability to save to the uttermost those who keep coming to Him, will bring His keeping power into play in our lives.

2. *Nullifying the Law of Marriage—Divorce*

> It hath been said, Whosoever shall put away his wife, let him give her a writing of divorcement: But I say unto you, That whosoever shall put away his wife, saving for the cause of fornication, causeth her to commit adultery: And whosoever shall marry her that is divorced committeth adultery (vv. 31–2).

When Jesus spoke these words the Jews had become lax in their interpretation of the Mosaic Law of divorce stated in Deut. 24:1. A woman could be divorced for so trivial a reason as burning her husband's dinner. As a result, the marriage relation had become very insecure. The same conditions obtain in many Moslem lands today with the result that many women who cherish high ideals are reluctant to marry. A thrice-repeated 'I divorce you' is sufficient to end the marriage contract. Our Lord's teaching aimed at correcting this abuse, and restoring marriage to a place of honour and security in the national life.

Among the Pharisees, one school contended that divorce was permissible 'for every cause' (Matt. 19:3 A.V.) or 'for any cause at all' (A.S.V.) That is, they permitted the widest latitude. Jesus on the contrary, said that divorce was permissible *for one cause only*—unchastity (Matt. 19:9). He made the necessity for fidelity in the married state absolute.

Whatever else may be misty on the question of divorce, there can be no mistaking Christ's emphasis, or His ideal for Christian marriage. This is not the place for an extended treatise on divorce, but in summary we can say that Jesus taught:

1. Divorce was never God's will, but it was permitted under the Mosaic Law as a concession to the obduracy of the human heart (Matt. 19:8).

2. There is only one valid ground for divorce—unchastity.

3. Except for this cause, marriage as a divinely sanctioned institution, is dissolved only by death.

4. Remarriage of the innocent partner is not prohibited.

5. One who divorces the other partner in cases where there has been no unchastity, is guilty of a grievous sin.

6. The offending party who remarries while his or her spouse is alive, thus becomes guilty of adultery.

7. These restrictions were designed to preserve the sanctity of home and family.

It remains to comment on one obscure sentence in this paragraph: 'Whoever shall put away his wife saving for the cause of fornication, *causeth her to commit adultery.*' What does this statement mean? On the face of it, this translation does not make sense. How does a man cause an innocent woman to commit adultery by divorcing her? Surely that is in her hands alone. As well say that a man is caused to steal by having his goods stolen.

William Hendriksen offers a satisfying explanation.[8] Jesus is speaking here of the sin of the man, not of the innocent woman. She has done no wrong. It is he who has sinned and committed adultery by his remarriage.

The key to the problem appears to lie in the fact that *the verb is passive* in form, indicating something suffered, not something committed. So eminent an authority as Thayer asserts that there is no reason why it should be translated as active here.

In view of this, Hendriksen submits this translation 'But I say unto you, that everyone who puts away his wife, saving for fornication, causes her to *suffer* adultery'—not to commit it—'and he who shall marry her that has been put away, *makes himself guilty of adultery*'. She suffers the wrong. He does the wrong.

The thought is that the innocent wife is stigmatised and suffers as though she were an adultress, with all the resultant distress and disgrace. It is the innocent party who suffers.

The importance in our day of maintaining these standards with the utmost care, cannot be overstressed. Christ's requirement of His disciples was absolute chastity outside marriage and absolute fidelity within marriage.

'Here speaks the flaming heart of Infinite Purity, loving the bairns, taking care of succeeding generations. The sin that curses society is a sin of the heart . . . He is talking in the interests of boys and girls, of what they are to be when they touch the larger life'.[4]

SIMPLE TRUTHFULNESS VERSUS FORBIDDEN SWEARING

> Again ye have heard that it hath been said by them of old time. Thou shalt not foreswear thyself, but shalt perform to the Lord thine oaths: But I say unto you, swear not at all; neither by heaven; for it is God's throne: Nor by the earth, for it is his footstool: Neither shalt thou swear by thy head, because thou canst not make one hair white or black. But let your communication be, Yea, yea; Nay, nay: for whatsoever is more than these cometh of sin (vv. 33–7).

This third example of the new standard emphasises the necessity of reverence for truth. It relates to the third commandment which enjoins: 'Thou shalt not take the name of the Lord thy God in vain'. The Master reviews the complicated system of oaths and swearing which the Pharisees had woven around this commandment, and elucidates its true meaning.

An oath is a solemn affirmation or declaration, made with an appeal to God for the truth of what is affirmed. In our Lord's day, oaths were in very frequent use but they tended to be trivial and flippant. The Jews used the most sacred language for the most trifling occasions, and with the minimum of sincerity. Their selection of oaths was more often with a view to evasion rather than performance.

As this paragraph illustrates, swearing and oaths had developed into a highly complex system, as it is to this day in some Moslem lands. In His exposition of the inner meaning of the commandment, Jesus stressed the fact that the law of truthfulness is violated just as effectively by the equivocal formula as by deliberate untruth.

If it is asked why oaths and swearing have become necessary, the answer is, because of the deceitfulness of the human heart. 'All men are liars', the psalmist said in his haste. If this were not so, oaths would be unnecessary. They are employed because men are unable to believe the simple, unadorned statements of their fellows. And yet is it not true that the stronger the assertion, the greater the suspicion of insincerity or evasion? Peter's vociferous oaths were only a cloak to cover his craven denial. In any case, oaths mean nothing to liars, as any court official can bear witness. If lies were not so universal, oaths would have no meaning.

Two classes of oaths were recognised by the Pharisees. First, oaths which specifically mentioned the name of God. These were considered irrevocably binding. Second, oaths in which the name of God could be implied, but was not actually spoken. These were not binding.

This casuistry left any amount of room for evading

the obligations of a commitment. The oath was binding or not binding, according to the sacredness of the object sworn by. This in turn gave birth to the conception of *degrees of truth and truthfulness*, a concept which is entirely repugnant to the teaching of Christ and the tenor of Scripture.

Truth does not permit of degrees. There are no greys in truth, only black or white. One statement cannot be more true than another—it is either absolutely true or completely false. There are no gradations in truth, and God refuses to be made partner to a false or evasive statement.

The Jews, who were experts in splitting hairs about binding and non-binding oaths, interpreted the law in such a way as to allow themselves the greatest licence. So long as God's name, though implied, was not actually stated, they were free to break their oath—yet it imparted an air of sanctity to their affirmation or promise.

Jesus ruthlessly exposed their duplicity and chicanery. They would not swear by the name of God if they did not wish to be bound by their oath, for the Law said 'Thou shalt not swear by my name falsely' (Lev. 19:15). But they would swear by heaven, or by Jerusalem with all their sacred associations. Jesus said to them in effect: 'God is everywhere, even if His name is not mentioned. If you swear by heaven, His throne is established there. If you swear by earth, that is His footstool. If you swear by Jerusalem, that is God's city. Hence an oath sworn by any of these is an oath sworn by the God who dwells there.' They must, therefore, abjure not only actual perjury, but all those allegedly non-binding oaths.

Court Oaths not Prohibited

By the unequivocal command, 'Swear not at all', Jesus was not making a blanket condemnation of all oaths, as some have maintained. His object was to stop the profanity and untruthfulness that was so rife. In point of fact, he was not referring to the secular realm but to the moral and spiritual. If these were corrected, the secular would also be affected.

Our Lord's own actions confirmed that He was not condemning all oaths, for He did not refuse to be put on oath : 'And the high priest said unto him, I adjure thee by the living God, that thou tell us whether thou be Christ the Son of God. Jesus saith to him, Thou hast said...' (Matt. 26:63–4).

Paul's attitude was consistent with that of his Master. He called on God to witness to the truth of his statements. 'God is my witness how greatly I long after you all' (Phil. 1:8; 2 Cor. 1:23). Indeed, God, 'because he could swear by no greater, sware by himself' (Heb. 6:13).

These sacred precedents afford assurance that the use of an oath is not forbidden. There is no reason, therefore, why a Christian should have qualms about taking an oath in court, when the Lord Himself had none.

To summarise the significance of our Lord's teaching on this subject for us today :

1. Truth is absolute. There can be no degrees of truthfulness. There is no such thing as a half-truth, it is a whole lie. There is no such thing as a white lie. It is as black as the hell in which it was spawned.

2. There cannot be separate secular and sacred compartments in the life of the disciple. God is everywhere and always present.

3. Evasion of the obligations of a promise or undertaking by the use of a second-class oath, is unworthy of a citizen of the Kingdom.

4. The ordinary conversation of the disciple, as well as his formal undertakings, are to be simple and unsophisticated. His 'Yes' and 'No', his simple promise, are to him to be as inviolable as the most sacred oath.

5. His character is to be such that oaths are superfluous. His word is his bond and others know it. Such fidelity to truth is a Christian characteristic.

71

6. Jesus lifts *all* conversation to the level of the sacredness of an oath. Integrity of speech is to be absolute. Social evasions, conventional suppressions, ego-boosting exaggerations, insincerity in promises, flippancy in sacred things, have no place in the Christian's vocabulary.

7. In this era of deception and falsehood, when politics, advertising, business and even ordinary conversation are shot through with insincerity if not with blatant lying, when superlatives have lost all meaning, obedience to this injunction of the Master will mark the disciple as unmistakably not of this world.

NON-RETALIATION VERSUS FORBIDDEN VENGEANCE

> Ye have heard that it hath been said, an eye for eye and a tooth for a tooth: But I say unto you that ye resist not evil (vv. 38–9a).

The fourth example of the new standard of the Kingdom relates to the law of vengeance and retaliation— *lex talionis* as it is called—the law of tit for tat. It is stated in Exod. 21 : 22–5.

> If men strive . . . and if any mischief follow, then thou shalt give life for life, eye for eye, tooth for tooth, hand for hand, foot for foot, burning for burning, wound for wound, stripe for stripe.

This is far from the New Testament ethic, but it was suited to the age and stage of civilisation in which it was given, and it was a great advance on current practice.

This is the principle of hard rigid justice, the judicial principle of adequate compensation for injury suffered. It was an early anticipation of the principle underlying our Workers' Compensation Acts. It was not intended to authorise men to take redress into their hands. On the contrary, it was designed to take vengeance out of private hands, and put it in the hands of the constituted authority. It was a direction to them to inflict penalties and exact compensation precisely equivalent to offences.

This principle was incorporated into both Greek and Roman law, and was followed by the Jews. In ears which have become accustomed to the accents of grace, it may sound harsh and severe, but it was a vast improvement on the unrestrained vengeance and vendettas of those days.

Then the common attitude was, 'If he has taken one of my eyes in the fight, then I will gouge out both of his.' It will be seen that the old Law permitted taking vengeance up to a point, but restricted it by fixing exact compensation for injury suffered. What Jesus demanded was not limitation, or even moderation, but total abolition of vengeance, and instead, exhibition of the spirit of love and forbearance. The Old Testament checked vengeance. Jesus forbade revenge.

The Master's words were directed not against the Law *per se*, but at the perversion of it by the Pharisees. They exploited it to give colour of right to their personal vendettas and acts of revenge. But the purpose of the *lex talionis* was not to legalise acts of private vengeance. It related to the public administration of the Law by the appropriate authorities.

Principle of Non-resistance

The clause 'Resist not evil' has had widely differing interpretations and applications. The rendering 'Do not resist one who is evil' (R.S.V.) is probably the better translation.

Some have taken this to mean that a Christian is not to resist any kind of evil at any time. But this obviously cannot be its significance. What of the One who gave the command? Did He so interpret it in His actions? Did He not resist evil in a most vigorous manner when, with whip of cords, He drove the traders from the Temple?

This is not a directive for nations, as is maintained by some sincere and ardent pacifists. It is not a blanket condemnation of all wars. That Jesus is not speaking about states or nations, is clear from the context. Non-retaliation in cases of personal wrong suffered is His subject. Nations as such are not in the Kingdom. There is no such thing as a Christian nation. Of the four illustrations He cites, all are on the level of the individual, not of the nation.

This command does not make all acts of war unconditionally wrong. Under the old order, God commanded Israel, as an act of moral surgery, to exterminate the corrupt, demon-worshipping Canaanites, in the interests of the moral and spiritual health of the whole world. Self-defence is not prohibited in the Old Testament (Exod. 22:2). Romans 13:3-5 implies the right of governments to wage war against aggression. One cannot help but admit, however, that the wars of our day are so complex in origin, motive and execution, that variant views on their justification are inevitable.

Nor does it prohibit all action against evil men, to maintain the social order, or in the interests of justice. For example, would it be wrong for a Christian to go to the aid of a policeman engaged in his law-enforcing duties? 'There is no authority except from God, and those that exist have been instituted by God,' wrote Paul. It cannot therefore be wrong for the Christian to support the authority in discharging his divinely appointed responsibilities, 'for he is the servant of God to execute his wrath on the wrongdoer'.

The prohibition, 'Resist not evil' is obviously not absolute, but it does teach clearly that the citizen of the Kingdom must not resist *personal* wrong in a vindictive and unforgiving spirit. When personal feelings are under control, it may be right to take action against the

74

evil man. Failure to act might be interpreted as condoning the evil.

We must not take the law into our own hands. Paul gives the Christian outlook with crystal clarity:

> Never pay back evil for evil to anyone . . . Never take your own revenge, beloved, but leave room for the wrath of God, for it is written, Vengeance is mine, I will repay, saith the Lord . . . Do not be overcome by evil, but overcome evil with good' (Rom. 12:17, 19–21 N.A.S.V.).

Writing of William Ewart Gladstone, one of Britain's greatest Prime Ministers, and a practising Christian, his biographer said:

> Of how few who have lived for more than sixty years in the full sight of their countrymen, and have as party leaders been exposed to angry and sometimes spiteful criticism, can it be said that there stands against them no malignant word and no vindictive act! This was due not perhaps entirely to natural sweetness of disposition, but rather to self-control, and to a certain largeness of soul which would not condescend to anything mean and petty.[5]

The principle of non-resistance to and non-retaliation for personal injuries has been stated. Now it is to be illustrated. Jesus selected four pertinent situations common to contemporary life, in order to show that much more is expected from the disciple than from other men.

Jesus poses a question at the close of this section which underlies a great deal of the teaching of the Sermon:

> If ye love them that love you, what reward have ye? Do not even the publicans the same? And if

ye salute your brethren only, *what do ye more* than others? Do not even the publicans so? (vv. 46–7).

There is to be an observable difference in the actions and reactions of the Christian. He is to do more than others. The difficult circumstances in which he may find himself, afford a unique opportunity of displaying other-worldly grace and graciousness, and this will commend His Master, who always did more than others. Tennyson paid this tribute to Archbishop Cranmer:

> *To do him wrong was to beget*
> *A kindness from him; for his heart was rich—*
> *Of such fine mould that if you sowed therein*
> *The seed of Hate, it blossomed Charity.*

1. *Reaction to Insult*

> Whosoever shall smite thee on the right cheek, turn to him the other also (v. 39b).

The acuteness of the insult is more apparent when one realises that to the Jew, being slapped in the face is the equivalent of our spitting in the face. A. M. Hunter sees in our Lord's remark an element of humour that may well be there. 'Has someone slapped you on the right cheek? Well, you have another!'[6]

He also points out that 'according to the rabbis, a blow with the back of the hand, which would normally land on your opponent's right cheek, was twice as bad as hitting him with the flat of your hand'. This was therefore the ultimate in insult, and one is to turn the other cheek!

In point of fact Jesus did not literally turn his other cheek when the officer struck Him with his hand. Instead, He courteously but firmly claimed His legal

76

right to fair trial. 'If I have spoken wrongly, bear witness of the wrong; but if I have spoken rightly, why strike ye Me?' (John 18:22, 23).

While it is true that Jesus did not obey the exact letter of His own injunction, by His controlled and dignified bearing He did fulfil its spirit. He did not lose His temper and vilify the officer who struck Him, or strike back at him. He simply asserted His right to fair trial. Similarly, when charged with being a glutton and a drunkard, He did not retort in kind. He offered no retaliation or reciprocal reviling.

Paul's reaction in somewhat similar circumstances stands in strong contrast:

> Paul earnestly beholding the council said, Men and brethren, I have lived in good conscience before God unto this day. And the high priest Ananias commanded them that stood by to smite him on the mouth. Then said Paul unto him, God shall smite thee, thou whited wall: for sittest thou to judge me after the law, and commandest me to be smitten contrary to the law? (Acts 23:1-4).

While one may have a secret sympathy with Paul's instinctive reaction, the contrast with that of his Master manifests the glory of the Son of God.

The point of the illustration is, that the disciple is to be willing to submit to a second insult rather than retaliate. 'Better to suffer wrong twice than to do wrong once.' If he insults you, let him repeat it, and meet his insult with Christian love. To this attitude he will be able to find no answer.

> What if He hath decreed that I shall first
> Be tried in humble state and things adverse,
> By tribulations, injuries, insults,
> Contempts and scorns, and snares, and violence?
> John Milton

77

2. Reaction to Inequity

> If any man will sue thee at law and take away thy coat, let him have thy cloak also (v. 40).

The crux of this illustration is that the cloak was the more valuable and costly garment, which frequently served as a blanket at night. In case of debt, a creditor could seize the cloak as a pledge, but the law made compassionate provision for one who so used it: 'If you take your neighbour's garment in pledge, you shall restore it to him before the sun goes down' (Exod. 22:26).

With this background in mind, the full implications of Christ's demand become apparent. Here, as elsewhere in the Sermon, it is not necessarily the literal fulfilment He is requiring, for He is enunciating principles to govern all behaviour, rather than formulating rules for individual circumstances. What He is saying is that the disciple should be willing to give up, not only as much as the law demands, but even that which it has no right to take. He is to do more than others. This is indeed a hard saying.

It should be noted that there is no question of actual theft involved, or this attitude would amount to complicity with evil. The issue involved in this illustration, as in the last, is that of non-resistance to personal wrong. The Christian will not initiate a law suit to redress his wrongs or obtain his rights. He would sooner suffer himself to be defrauded, as Paul enjoined (1 Cor. 6:7), leaving the issue in the competent hands of his heavenly Father.

At the crucifixion, the soldiers took Jesus's coat, and He let them have His cloak also. His only retaliation was a prayer for their forgiveness. He did not resist evil, but overcame evil with good.

3. Reaction to Imposition

> Whosoever shall compel thee to go a mile, go with
> him twain (v. 41).

This illustration has as its source a practice of the Per-
sian postal service, which was carried over into the
Roman administration. The King of Persia used to
station mounted couriers at fixed points, to transmit
messages one to the other. If a man was passing one of
these posts, the courier was empowered to compel him
to go to another post to perform an errand for the
King. So was it under Rome. If an official engaged on
state business required assistance, he could conscript a
passer-by into his service for the next stage of the jour-
ney. But the legal limit for such conscripted service was
one mile. He had no power to demand further service.

What Jesus said was, in effect, 'although he has no
power to compel you to go more than one mile, sur-
prise him by cheerfully volunteering to go a second!
This totally unprecedented attitude will convince him
that you are actuated by different and higher motives
than others.'

For us the lesson is that we are not to rest content
with doing our bare duty, but to do more and do it
gladly. We are not to greedily grasp our legal rights
and insist on them, but to be as our Lord, 'For he, who
had always been God by nature, did not cling to his
prerogative as God's equal, but stripped himself of all
privilege by consenting to be a slave . . .' (Phil. 2:6
Phillips).

Nor are we to resent public claims upon our time or
resources, but rather to welcome these opportunities
of serving others, even those who have injured us. It
has been suggested that if going the first mile was rendering to Caesar the things that are Caesar's, going the
second mile is rendering to God the things that are God's.
It is a God-like action.

In summarising the teaching of these three illustrations, note that the first is concerned with insult to the person, the second with the rights of property, and the third with compulsory public service. In each case the attitude is non-resistance. The disciple is to submit to the insult, relinquish the cloak and go the extra mile.

But more than that—for the disciple is to do more than others—the other cheek is to be offered, the more costly garment surrendered, and the load carried for a second mile. He can disarm evil, not by retaliation, but by readiness to submit to more, and that without resentment. This is truly a heavenly standard.

4. Reaction to Indigence

> Give to him that asketh of thee, and from him who would borrow of thee, turn not away (v. 42).

Jesus has two classes in view—the beggar and the borrower. To those who have lived in countries where abject poverty and unabashed begging are an integral part of life, this injunction poses a nagging problem. Few questions cause more soul-searching for the sympathetic person. To give, or not to give? That is the question.

Does Jesus here advocate literal indiscriminate giving to all and sundry? As elsewhere in the Sermon, at first glance it appears to be so; but we must constantly remind ourselves that Jesus is not legislating, or reducing the Christian life to a set of wooden rules. This is the very error He is aiming to correct. He is laying down broad spiritual principles to be applied to differing situations as they arise. The principle involved in this illustration is not that of indiscriminate giving, but self-sacrificing generosity.

'This is one of the clearest instances of the necessity of accepting the spirit and not the letter of the Lord's commands (see vv. 32, 34, 38). Not only does indiscriminate almsgiving do little but injury to society, but the words must embrace much more than almsgiving.'

It is related of the godly William Law, whose *Serious Call to a Devout Life* exercised a great influence in past days and is still in circulation, that he used to give away £2,500 a year to beggars, in his backyard—an enormous sum in those days. But the record is that all he achieved by his open-handed charity was to demoralise the neighbourhood! If a practice is to be judged by its fruits, then indiscriminate giving does not have much in its favour.

The Law made provision for the generous treatment of the needy brother. 'If there be among you a poor man of one of thy brethren, thou shalt not harden thy heart, nor shut thy hand from thy poor brother: but thou shalt open thy hand wide to him, and shalt surely lend to him *sufficient for his need*' (Deut. 15:7, 8). Not necessarily all he asks, but all he needs, is the principle.

But in their giving and lending, the Jews always took into account the probable effect upon the recipient. One does not give a knife to a baby, however loudly it screams for it. Is one to give money to an alcoholic and watch him go into the bar and exchange it for the liquor that damns his body and soul?

Indiscriminate giving encourages laziness in some and demoralises others. Bishop Gore stresses the necessity for inquiry being made into the merits of the case, before the gift or loan is made. This need not stifle the generous impulse, but it will sift the deserving cases from the undeserving. At the same time it will eliminate the professional beggar who is easily discouraged when he understands that inquiry will be made, and will seek other pastures. To the deserving man, making inquiries will hold no terrors.

The amount we should give will be gauged by our ability, and the circumstances of the case. We should err on the generous side, even at cost to ourselves. We should be as open-handed to those who have no claim on us as to those who have.

Augustine tendered this advice as to the extent of our generosity: 'We are not told to give everything we are asked for, but to everyone that asks, even if there is no prospect of a return.'

On this point E. Stanley Jones has this to say:

His real need may be money—then give him, not necessarily *all* that he asks, for that might conflict with the legitimate askings of one's own family— but give to him. He may ask for money, and you may see that merely to give money is a cheap and easy and ruinous way out. You must give him more —you must give him the disposition, if possible, to stand on his own feet and be self-respecting.[8]

We are not to spurn a brother in distress, or turn a deaf ear to his plea, even if he has wronged us. We are to be merciful to him as God has been merciful to us. An unfeeling refusal to relieve a brother in need is entirely contrary to the spirit of the Kingdom.

IMPARTIAL LOVE VERSUS FORBIDDEN HATRED

Ye have heard that it hath been said, Thou shalt love thy neighbour and hate thine enemy. But I say unto you, Love your enemies, bless them that curse you, do good to them that hate you, and pray for those that despitefully use and persecute you, that ye may be the children of your Father which is in heaven: For he maketh his sun to rise on the evil and on the good, and sendeth rain on the just and on the unjust. (vv. 43–5).

The last illustration of the new standard of His Kingdom imposes on the disciple the humanly impossible requirement of loving the enemy who hates, reviles and persecutes him. This incredible law of love has been termed the concentrated expression of the Christian ethic. Of course we do not *like* the enemy who persecutes and vilifies us, but that is not to prevent us from loving him. Affinity or aversion is quite irrelevant to this exotic species of love.

In current usage, the word 'love' has been soiled and debased by its almost exclusive association with the romantic and the erotic. Love is conceived of almost entirely in terms of the emotional. This element is of necessity present, but it is by no means predominant.

The Greek *agape* used here is 'the love which loves despite the repulsiveness of its object, and is contrasted with *eros* which is love elicited by the attractive qualities of the loved one'. It is moral love as distinguished from personal affection. It is the attitude of sustained and undiscourageable love towards both friend and enemy. A love which does not demand or desire, but gives; that goes on loving, whatever the insult or injury suffered.

This love is not *mere emotion*, but involves volition and action as well. It must find expression in acts of love for deserving and undeserving alike. It is the love of God as seen in John 3 : 16. In this verse it is the volitional rather than the emotional element in God's love which is highlighted. God's love for men who were His undeserving enemies, moved His will to the infinitely costly action of surrendering His only Son to death on a cross for their redemption.

The most important thing is not what we feel but what we *will*. To give His Son to such a shameful and agonising death as crucifixion, was the last thing God would *feel* like doing, but He willed to do it for our sake.

Nor is this a love that comes *unsought*, like falling in love with someone; it involves a definite activity of the will. This is how it is possible for the Christian to love someone he doesn't even like. He may not feel like loving him, but he chooses to do so, and ultimately his feelings will follow his will. It does not mean that we will have the same kind of love for our enemies as for our dear friends. There is a different word for that love.

The Jews apparently drew the inference from the Old Testament command, that because one must love one's neighbour, one is therefore at liberty to hate one's enemies—a glaring *non sequitur*. Hence our Lord's quotation: 'Ye have heard it hath been said, Thou shalt love thy neighbour and hate thine enemy . . .' Bengel makes this acid comment on their attitude: 'As if the one were a legitimate inference from the other, instead of a detestable gloss.'

Actually the Law nowhere said, 'Hate your enemy'; nor did it sanction such an attitude. It was a Pharisaic perversion which Jesus utterly repudiated. The words of Paul in Rom. 12:20, 'Therefore if thine enemy hunger, feed him, if he thirst, give him drink . . .', are simply a quotation from the Old Testament (Prov. 22:21) which they conveniently ignored.

The Pharisees had their own method of escaping the obligations of such words. One of their evasive maxims was: 'If a Jew see a Gentile fallen into the sea, let him by no means lift him out thence. It is written, "Thou shalt not rise up against the blood of thy neighbour", but this man is not thy neighbour.'[9] With such an outlook it is not surprising that the Romans charged the Jews with hatred of the human race.

Who is My Neighbour?

To this question the Jew would answer, 'My fellow-Israelite.' But Jesus shattered this conception in His parable of the Good Samaritan. By it He lifted love to one's neighbour far above the Jewish limitation of it to one's compatriots. My neighbour is anyone who needs my assistance, be he friend or enemy. 'Whoever stands closest to a man in need has a neighbourly duty to him.'

Who is My Enemy?

The question is answered by the Lord: 'Them that curse you . . . hate you . . . despitefully use you . . . persecute you' (v. 44). He not only describes the enemy but prescribes the reaction of the disciple. He is to *bless* those who curse him and wish him evil. He is to *do good*, to those who hate him. He is to *pray* for them that persecute him. This is the response of Christian love.

Our Lord was the best example of His own teaching. Peter tells us that, 'Christ also suffered for us, leaving us an example that ye should follow his steps . . . who, when he was reviled, reviled not again; when he suffered, he threatened not' (1 Pet. 2 : 21, 23).

Admittedly this is a desperately high standard. As Augustine put it: 'Good for good, evil for evil; that is natural. Evil for good; that is devilish. Good for evil; that is divine.' But it this very fact that provides the disciple with his greatest opportunity of displaying his other-worldly love of the Master.

Our attitudes and actions are to display and reflect our sonship: 'That ye may be the children of your Father which is in heaven' (v. 45). This will be seen especially in the impartiality of our love. We will exhibit the family likeness, for the impartial God bestows the blessings of sun and rain on evil and good alike.

As our Father does not discriminate between the deserving and undeserving in His providential dealings with men, so must His sons be in their dealings with their enemies.

There is nothing wonderful in loving those that love us. 'What do ye more than others?' Jesus asks. Tyndale translates the question: 'What singuler thinge doo ye?' Our love is not to be regulated by likes and dislikes. The Master expects from His disciples such conduct as can be explained only in terms of the supernatural.

What is it to be Perfect?

> Be ye therefore perfect, even as your Father in heaven is perfect (v. 48).

This verse has been the subject of much misunderstanding and much verbal debate. It summarises and crystallises what He has been teaching, and to understand its meaning it must be borne in mind that these words were spoken in connection with the duty of loving one's enemies. It is in this context that it must be interpreted.

From the meaning of the word 'perfect', and its context, it can be asserted that Jesus was not here speaking about abstract philosophical perfection. Nor was He speaking of absolute sinlessness, for He had earlier in the Sermon stated that one element of the blessedness of the citizen of the Kingdom was that he mourned, hungered and thirsted after righteousness, which obviously was not yet attained. The perfection here envisaged relates back to the perfection of the Father's love (v. 45).

The word *teleios*, here translated 'perfect', is used elsewhere of relative perfection, as of adults compared with children, and carries the idea of maturity, completeness. A thing is perfect in this sense when it reaches maturity, when it fulfils the purpose for which it was designed. Interpreted here in its context, the word implies that as the character of God is sacrificial and self-imparting love, so the disciple is 'perfect' when he reproduces that love in word and action. He is then mature, and fulfilling the purpose for which God created him in His own image.

A love which embraces friends but not enemies is not perfect, it is immature. Like God who sends sun and rain on good and bad alike, we are to be impartial in our love—omitting no group, loving enemies as well as friends.

Love of this character is a sheer impossibility apart from divine aid. Only the imparted grace of God can empower us to scale these dizzy heights. With Augustine we are forced to cry, 'O God, give what Thou commandest, then command what Thou wilt.'

And this is exactly what God has done for us, 'because the love of God *has been poured out* within our hearts, through the Holy Spirit who was given unto us' (Rom. 5:5 N.A.S.V.). Through the Spirit's agency, we have been made recipients of the Father's incredible love. It is the Spirit's delight to reproduce in us 'the fruit of the Spirit which is love'.

1. *Keswick Week* (London, Marshall, Morgan and Scott, 1903), p. 66.

2. Jamieson, Faussett and Brown, *Commentary* (London, Oliphants, 1961), p. 902.

3. Hendriksen, *The Sermon on the Mount*, p. 95.

4. G. Campbell Morgan, *The Gospel of Matthew* (London, Oliphants), p. 57.

5. James Bryce, *Studies in Contemporary Biography.*

6. Hunter, *Design for Life*, p. 54.

7. Robertson, *Word Pictures in the New Testament*, p. 49.

8. E. Stanley Jones, *The Christ of the Mount* (London, Hodder and Stoughton, 1931), p. 143.

9. See Tristram, *Eastern Customs in Bible Lands.*

7

The Sincerity of the Disciple's Motive

Matthew 6 : 1–18

Beware of practising your righteousness before men to be noticed by them; otherwise you have no reward with your Father who is in heaven (6 : 1 A.S.V.).

SECRECY VERSUS FORBIDDEN OSTENTATION

In the previous section of the Sermon, Jesus enunciated a general principle, and then elucidated its meaning by five illustrations. He follows the same pattern here. The above verse is the general principle which He proceeds to illustrate by three acts of visible devotion—giving, praying and fasting. These were three specimens of the Pharisaic 'righteousness', as it was called. (Note that the word translated 'alms' in the A.V. is correctly rendered 'righteousness' in the N.A.S.V.)

Jesus here warns His disciples of a twofold peril. First, performing acts of devotion 'to be noticed by men'—ostentation and self-advertisement. Second, failing to maintain in private the standard of devotion professed in public—hypocrisy. They must not do 'as the hypocrites do'.

Keep up appearances; there lies the test;
The world will give thee credit for the rest;
Outward be fair, however foul within;
Sin if thou wilt; but then, in secret sin.
The maxim's into common favour grown,
Vice is no longer vice unless 'tis known.

Charles Churchill

That this same principle is applicable to all three activities mentioned by the Lord can be seen by the thrice-repeated refrain: 'Verily they have their reward.' Their professed acts of devotion were a theatrical performance, designed to win the applause of the audience. Our word 'theatrical' would capture the idea of the word used in the clause, 'to be noticed by men'. They looked for applause, and they received it. The account is closed.

The fundamental lesson of this paragraph is that the disciple's life is to be lived primarily in the presence of God—'thy Father, who seeth in secret', and only secondarily before men. While not insensitive to the presence of his fellow men, the true disciple sets greater store on the approval of God than on the passing applause of his contemporaries.

The Reward Motive

This raises the whole question of the validity of the idea of reward in the Christian life, and the crucial importance of motive in our actions.

An Indian critic brought this objection against the gospel: 'The bottom has dropped out of reward morality; so Christianity and Christian missions founded on reward morality cease to grip the mind of this age that demands a higher basis for morality.'[1] It was obviously his opinion that morality based on an expectation of reward was very poorly motivated.

It is, of course, true that a man who is good only because it pays to be good is not good at all. But on the other hand, if the idea of reward is invalid, if the end of the evil man is the same as that of the good man, would it not mean that goodness is a matter of indifference?

Two facts must be borne in mind. First, that Jesus, far from disparaging the idea of reward, seemed to take it for granted. He did not condemn the prospect of a reward as an unworthy motive, but only seeking it from the wrong source. In our giving, praying or fasting, we may do it for God's glory or for our own, but either one cancels out the other.

If we take the ground that anticipation of reward is immoral or unspiritual, we would appear to be more spiritual than the Lord Himself. In the Hebrews letter it was written of Him, 'Who for the joy that was set before him, endured the cross, despising the shame, and is set down at the right hand of God' (12:2). This is plainly the anticipation of compensation for suffering on earth.

Then, too, the idea of reward and punishment is inherent in our very nature, 'Those who consider reward ignoble,' said Bishop Gore,[2] 'ignore indestructible and necessary instincts in human nature. We cannot separate love for God from a desire to find our happiness in God. This is inseparable from personality. We must crave for ultimate satisfaction, recognition, approval, but we must seek it in the right direction—from God.'

As to the nature of the rewards God extends to His children, they are not material but spiritual. To those whose aim it is to win the praise of men, the rewards God offers would be singularly unattractive. They are appreciated only by the spiritual man. Holy living brings it own reward in the present, in the consciousness of divine approval.

Conduct is always rewarded according to its inspiring motive. The true criterion of the eternal value of an act is the quality of the motive that prompted it. In no sense is the reward a *quid pro quo*. It can never be earned by any human achievement. It is the expression of the pure, overflowing generosity of God towards those who seek His glory above the praise of men.

Each of these three visible manifestations of a man's devotion—giving, praying, fasting—is singularly susceptible to unworthy motivation. One can give alms without a thought or care for the recipients, but only to enhance one's reputation for generosity. One can pray, and at the same time be more concerned about the impression the prayer makes on the audience, than on its acceptability to the God to whom it is ostensibly offered. One can discipline oneself by fasting, not for the spiritual benefit to be derived from the discipline, but to enhance one's prestige and reputation for holiness.

In each case the estimable act is vitiated by the discreditable motive. Not that those who so act do not receive a reward, for Jesus said, 'Verily they have their reward'. But all they receive is what they worked for and desired—the transient and empty praise of men. There is nothing more to come to them from God. They have received payment in full.

ALMSGIVING—GENEROSITY TO ONE'S NEIGHBOUR

> Therefore when thou doest thine alms, do not sound a trumpet before thee, as the hypocrites do in the synagogues and in the streets, that they may have glory of men. Verily I say unto you, they have their reward. But when thou doest alms let not thy left hand know what thy right hand doeth: that thine alms may be in secret: and thy Father which seeth in secret himself shall reward thee openly (vv. 2–4).

Giving of alms, i.e. something given gratuitously to relieve the poor, is taken for granted by the Master as a natural expression of Christian love. 'When thou doest thine alms', not 'If'. The fact is taken for granted, but heed must be paid to the motive and manner in which the alms are given.

The exact significance of 'Do not sound a trumpet before thee' is not certain, as there seems to be no record of such a practice. However, two interesting possibilities have been advanced.

Cyril of Alexandria saw in it a reference to the practice of almsgivers sounding a trumpet to summon beggars to come and receive the charity they were about to dispense, thus drawing attention to their meritorious act. But in reality the act was performed not for the benefit of the poor but for the aggrandisement of the donor.

The other suggestion is that the 'trumpet' refers to the thirteen money chests at the entrance to the Temple, into which the worshippers cast their gifts. From their shape they were called 'trumpets'. The ostentation and noise with which the money clanged into these receptacles sounded like the blare of a trumpet, calling attention to the gifts. And, after all, it was the favourable attention of the other worshippers that the donor was seeking.

Whether either of these explanations is the correct one or not, the meaning is not left in doubt. Our generosity is not to be advertised, even to bosom friends. Nor is it to be looked upon as an investment. That great Christian philanthropist Robert G. Le Tourneau used to say, 'If you give because it pays, then it won't pay.' We are not to go about letting others know that we are tithers. There is always the danger that our giving may degenerate into an oblique method of obtaining praise from men, rather than bringing glory to God.

The Element of Secrecy

The element of secrecy or privacy in our giving and praying and fasting—doing it as to God alone—is emphasised in the six-times repeated 'in secret'. Secrecy is of the essence of true piety. These exercises are not for human congratulation, and for this reason Jesus enjoined His disciples, 'When thou doest alms, let not thy left hand know what thy right hand doeth.'

Interpreting this figure with rigid literalism has led to situations which it neither envisages nor requires. The author remembers his father telling of a wealthy farmer who attended the same church, but who never put a cent in the collection plate. He was stigmatised as a skinflint, and as a result his testimony was ruined.

What lay behind his apparent meanness? Simply that he desired to render literal obedience to this exhortation of the Lord, whether he was misunderstood or not. The other church members were not to know that behind the scenes the farmer made an annual gift which amounted to more than the gifts of all the rest of the members combined. It was given on condition that there was the utmost secrecy. He felt that if he put the money in the public plate he would be letting his left hand know what his right hand did.

His motive was admirable, and God would have respect to that, but his misinterpretation of the verse cost him dear, and did not glorify God. That he had misunderstood the Lord's meaning is seen when it is recalled that, earlier in the Sermon, Jesus had urged His disciples so to live and witness that 'men may see your good works, and glorify your Father which is in heaven' (5 : 16). But are not these two injunctions in conflict? Does not one emphasise publicity and the other secrecy?

The solution lies in the fact that there are two Greek words for 'see'. One signifies knowledge gained from information supplied, and the other knowledge gleaned by perception, by noticing it. It is the latter word which is used in 5 : 16. We are not to supply others with information of our generosity, but there is no objection to our good works being noticed by others in the normal course of events. In fact, Jesus specifically said that one purpose of our good works is that glory might come to God through men seeing them.

Had the wealthy farmer acted normally and unostentatiously made a generous weekly offering, it would have brought glory to God, and others would have been stimulated by his example. A. B. Bruce's pungent advice is relevant: 'Show when tempted to hide, hide when tempted to show.'

It is not without significance that, right at the beginning of the dispensation of the Spirit, severe judgment fell on Ananias and Sapphira, who fell into both of the sins of which Jesus had warned. They gave the proceeds of the sale of their land in a spirit of ostentation, in order to obtain the praise of men. They acted as hypocrites by withholding part of the proceeds, while pretending that it was all. Thus early in the history of the Church, God underscored the seriousness of these two sins.

PRAYER—DEVOTION TO GOD

> When thou prayest, thou shalt not be as the hypocrites are: for they love to pray standing in the synagogues and in the corners of the streets, that they may be seen of men. Verily I say unto you, they have their reward. But thou, when thou prayest, enter into thy closet, and when thou hast shut the door, pray to thy Father which is in secret; and thy Father which seeth in secret shall reward thee openly (vv. 5–6).

Few subjects raise so many problems as the exercise of prayer. It is a paradox, blending complexity and simplicity. It is the simplest form of speech that infant lips can try, and yet the sublimest strains that reach the Majesty on high. It is as appropriate on the lips of the little child as on those of the aged philosopher. It is the ejaculation of a moment, and the attitude of a lifetime. It is an agony and an ecstasy. It is submissive and yet importunate. It can be focussed on a single objective and it can roam the world. It can be abject confession and rapt adoration.

We can therefore appropriately take on our lips the words of one of the greatest exponents of this art: 'We do not even know how we ought to pray.' But we can draw comfort from the fact that Paul was swift to add, 'But the Spirit comes to the aid of our weakness' (Rom. 8:26, 27 N.E.B.).

> The prayers I make will then be sweet indeed
> If Thou the Spirit give by which I pray:
> My unassisted heart is barren clay,
> That of itself can nothing feed:
> Of good and pious works Thou art the seed,
> That quickens only when Thou say'st it may:
> Unless Thou show to us Thine own true way
> No man can find it: Father, Thou must lead.

> Do Thou then, breathe those thoughts into
>   my mind
> By which such virtue may in me be bred
> That in Thy holy footsteps I may tread;
> The fetters of my tongue do Thou unbind,
> That I may have the power to sing of Thee,
> And sound Thy praises everlastingly.

Michael Angelo

Because prayer is so crucial and vital an element in the life of the believer our Lord accorded it both extensive and intensive treatment. Both negative and positive aspects are stressed. He first states the principles that govern prayer and then the pattern on which His disciples were to model their prayers was given. Later in the Sermon He again reverts to this theme.

Using as illustrations the hypocrites and the heathen, Jesus taught how not to pray.

The hypocrite, the play-actor, loved to pray in places

where he could be assured of a good audience to observe his devotion—the synagogue and the corners of the public squares. There he would strike a pious pose and say his prayers for all to see.

In this exhortation, Jesus is not condemning public prayer, but *private* prayer offered ostentatiously in *public places*. There is a place for public prayer, but public prayers cannot be offered in secret, and it is secret prayer to which He is referring.

The devout Jew, like the Moslem, observed his fixed times of prayer, which tended to become stereotyped and without heart. The appropriate liturgy would be recited repetitiously. The longer the prayer, the more devout the worshipper.

Jesus insisted that such praying was unacceptable to God. The essence of individual prayer is sincerity and secrecy, a tryst between the pray-er and his Father. Prayer is not for public notice but for private audience. One who would pray acceptably must withdraw from the presence of men and shut himself in with God.

The word 'openly' at the end of verse 4 is rightly omitted from most modern translations. Jesus does not extend the promise of public reward for private piety, but it will nevertheless ultimately have its reward.

The failure of the hypocrites can very easily become our failure. We too can be insincere and covet a reputation for piety. It was because Jesus knew this that He warned us, 'When thou prayest, be not as the hypocrites.'

To many in the crowded homes of Eastern lands the problem of finding a 'secret place' is acute. But, as the Master Himself has shown, the secrecy of prayer is available everywhere.

I need not leave the jostling crowd
Or wait till daily tasks are o'er
To fold my hands in secret prayer
Within the close shut closet door.

There is a viewless cloistered room
　　As high as heaven, as fair as day,
Where, though my feet may join the throng,
　　My soul can enter in and pray.
When I have banished wayward thoughts
　　Of sinful works the fruitful seed,
When folly wins my ear no more,
　　The closet door is shut indeed.
No human step approaching breaks
　　The blissful silence of the place.
No shadow steals across the 'light
　　That falls from my Redeemer's face!
And never through these crystal walls
　　The clash of life can pierce its way,
Nor ever can a human ear
　　Drink in the spirit words I say.
One, harkening, even cannot know
　　When I have crossed the threshold o'er,
For He alone who hears my prayer
　　Has heard the shutting of the door.

Author unknown

The prayers of the heathen, too, were unacceptable to God, because their conception of Him was erroneous. Instead of viewing Him as a loving Father, they conceived of Him as a vindictive, angry being who must be placated and appeased. So Jesus adds another warning:

But when ye pray, use not vain repetitions, as the heathen do; for they think that they shall be heard for their much speaking. Be not ye therefore like unto them; for your heavenly Father knoweth what things ye have need of before ye ask him (v. 6, 7).

'Vain repetitions' derives from the verb 'to stammer', with its connotation of the multiplication of words without the addition of meaning. This is what the prayers of the heathen were like. Obvious illustrations of such counterfeit prayer, are the prayer wheel of the Tibetan, the beads of the Buddhist, the Paternosters and Ave Marias of the Roman Catholic.

There is no value in mere repetition. 'Do not heap up empty phrases' is one translation of this sentence. But repetition itself is not invalid if it has both content and intent. All repetition in prayer is not banned, for it is recorded that Jesus 'prayed the third time, saying the same words' (Matt. 26:44). What He did repudiate was the superstitious and mechanical parroting of phrases. as though God could be cajoled into answering a mere spate of words.

Prayers are measured by their intensity and sincerity, not by their length or eloquence; by their childlike faith in the God to whom they are addressed.

We may not be guilty of the extremes of error into which the heathen fall in their praying, but do not some of our prayers fall into the same category? Cannot the repeated use of a liturgy, valuable in itself, degenerate into heaping up empty phrases unless we are on the alert? Are not many extempore prayers formal and heartless repetitions? And are not our public prayers beset with some of the same defects? We may easily be more concerned about its effect on the audience than its effectiveness with God. 'Be not ye therefore like unto the heathen,' was our Master's counsel.

Before turning to consider the Incomparable Prayer, the latter part of verse 8 demands notice.

Prayer is not for the purpose of informing God, 'for your heavenly Father knoweth what ye have need of before ye ask Him'. Then why the need of prayer? If God loves His children and knows their needs, surely He will supply them without the necessity of their plaguing Him with prayers for them!

The fact remains that the One who spoke these words also said later in the Sermon, '*Ask* and ye shall receive, *seek* and ye shall find, *knock* and it shall be opened to you.' In His eyes there was no incongruity between the two statements.

In an earthly family the father knows the needs of the children better than they do themselves. He plans to meet those needs to the very best of his ability. But does he not teach them to ask for things, not so much for his sake, as for the development of courtesy, thankfulness and thoughtfulness? A home where no one asked for anything or thanked others for them would not be a very attractive place to live.

Bishop Gore supplies at least a partial answer to the problem:

> Why is it, then, that God requires us to pray? The answer is quite a simple one. It is because God is our Father, and He wishes us to be trained in habits of conscious intercourse with Him. Therefore, just as many blessings which God wishes to give us are made dependent on our working for them, so many other blessings are made dependent on our regular and systematic asking.
>
> God wills to give them, but He wills to give them only if we ask Him, and this in order that the very necessity of continually holding intercourse with a personal God, and making request of Him, may train us in the habit of realising that we are sons of our heavenly Father.
>
> *The wisdom of this provision is best realised if we reflect how easily, when the practice of prayer is abandoned, the sense of a personal relation to God falls from our lives.*
>
> We are to pray, not to inform God, but to train ourselves in habits of personal intercourse with our Father who is in heaven.[3]

The Incomparable Prayer which our Lord gave to His disciples as a model is so important that a separate chapter is devoted to it, after the section on fasting.

> Moreover, when ye fast, be not as the hypocrites, of a sad countenance: for they disfigure their faces, that they may appear unto men to fast. Verily I say unto you, they have their reward. But thou, when thou fastest, anoint thy head, and wash thy face, that thou appear not unto men to fast, but unto Thy Father which is in secret: and thy Father which seeth in secret shall reward thee openly (v. 16–18).

Once again the principle stated in verse 1 is reiterated and applied to the third visible means of devotion—fasting.

In His exhortation Jesus did not condemn fasting, but only the ostentation and insincerity with which it was practised by the hypocrites, the play-actors who simulated an emotion they did not feel. They only played a part to gain a round of applause.

God takes no pleasure in disfigured or lugubrious faces. Using them as an example, Jesus warned His disciples against making their fasting an occasion for the parade of their piety. They were to present a joyous face to the public, and let their fasting be 'in secret', to God alone.

As Jesus used the word, fasting had reference to abstinence from food for a period, and for a spiritual purpose. This conception has largely gone out of fashion, and is little practised. 'Fasting of the mind', or 'fasting in spirit', has taken the place of abstinence from food. But would it not be equally consistent to speak of giving alms 'in spirit'? The result would not be very satisfying to the poor! Fasting could in a secondary sense include abstaining from anything legitimate in itself, for a spiritual purpose.

There is little doubt of what Jesus had in mind. Did He not commence His own ministry with a prolonged period of fasting? (Matt. 4:2). But it should be remembered at the same time that He was so unascetic in His manner of life that He was accused, falsely, of being a gluttonous man, and a drunkard.

He is here instructing His disciples in the spirit and manner of true fasting. 'Anoint thy head and wash thy face, that thou appear not unto men to fast.' He did not, however, enjoin fasting upon them, nor did He appoint any fast as part of the spiritual exercises of His Kingdom (Matt. 9:14; 18:18, 19). While not abolishing fasting, Jesus lifted it out of the legalism of the Old Covenant into the liberty of the New.

In a penetrating study of the subject, Dr H. W. Frost asserted that in the New Testament fasting was nowhere enjoined on the believer. He is at liberty to fast or not, as he chooses. Jesus neither commended nor condemned it. It is not a legalistic requirement, but a spontaneous spiritual reaction to special circumstances.

The fact is that not all Christians find fasting an aid to prayer. Some sincere and godly people known to the author have found it more of a hindrance than a help. They are so constituted that the lack of a minimum amount of food renders them unable to concentrate in prayer. There is no need for them to be in bondage. Let them do what best helps them to pray.

The idea that food produces carnality, while abstinence from food induces spirituality, has no biblical support. It is true that over-indulgence in food is not conducive to deep spirituality, but that is another matter. It was Paul's teaching that 'the Kingdom of God is not meat and drink, but righteousness, and peace, and joy in the Holy Spirit' (Rom. 4:17). 'Meat commendeth us not to God; for neither if we eat more are we the better; neither if we eat not are we the worse' (1 Cor. 8:8).

In other words, there is no merit in the fasting itself. It does not follow that so much fasting will produce so much in spiritual results, or in prayer answers. It is not an end in itself, but a means to an end. It is not to be observed on Fridays, but when God leads to it.

It appears from the New Testament that fasting is a matter in which there is complete liberty. And yet the fact remains that prayer with fasting has been the habit of many of the greatest saints in all ages. Many missionaries have testified that insoluble problems and impregnable situations have yielded to prayer with fasting. One does not usually fast unless one is deeply in earnest.

One obvious value of fasting is that it assists us to 'keep the body under and keep it in subjection' (1 Cor. 9:29). It is a practical acknowledgment of the supremacy of the spiritual over the sensual. Those who practise it in a spiritual manner and for spiritual ends state that the mind becomes unusually clear and vigorous. There is a noticeable spiritual quickening, and increased powers of concentration.

From the occasions with which it is associated in the New Testament it would seem that fasting is the natural outcome of preoccupation. Nowhere does it appear to be premeditated or prearranged.

Historically, as Dr Frost observes, it was usually associated with some strong emotion begotten by some matter of special spiritual concern. For example, the temptation of the Lord (Matt. 4:2); Cornelius praying to God for a revelation of His truth (Acts 10:30, 31); the Church leaders at Antioch, burdened for a lost world (Acts 13:1–3); Paul and Barnabas, concerned about appointing elders over the infant churches of Asia (Acts 14:23).

In the grip of an overmastering concern these men were led into a prolongation of prayer during which eating was a secondary consideration. To them the other issues were more important. The length of the fast was determined, not by a previous decision, but by the pressure of the heart-concern. When the burden lifted, the fasting ceased.

From the study of the relevant Scripture it emerges

that fasting was the outcome of (a) the challenge of a special temptation; (b) a deep yearning after a closer walk with God; (c) a great burden for the spread of the gospel in regions beyond; (d) spiritual travail for the upbuilding of the Church; (e) the exigencies of a stubborn situation (Matt. 17:21).

The life of Pastor Hsi,[4] Chinese saint and scholar, was a striking example of the validity and value of fasting. One who travelled with him wrote:

> Constantly, and in everything he dealt with God. In a very real way he dealt with Satan too. His conflict with the evil one at times was such that he would give himself to days of fasting and prayer. Even when travelling, I have known him fast for a whole day over some difficult matter that needed clearing up. That was always his resource—fast and pray . . . I have never seen one with so much influence over others.

1. Jones, *The Christ of the Mount*, p. 177.
2. Gore, *The Sermon on the Mount*, p. 106.
3. ibid., p. 119.
4. Mrs Howard Taylor, *Pastor Hsi* (London, China Inland Mission, 1900), pp. 166–7.

8

The Secrets of the Disciple's Prayer

Matthew 6 : 9–13

This most widely used of all religious formularies has suffered greatly at the hands of its friends. Some neglect it, some recite it heedlessly, and only a minority use it as the Lord intended.

In the verses immediately preceding the Prayer, Jesus warned of two perils which He foresaw would beset the use of it. They were not to pray as the hypocrites or as the heathen. The hypocrites reserved their praying for public, while the heathen heaped up empty phrases. It is these two things which have done most to rob the Prayer of its significance and blessing. It is reserved mainly for public recitation, and it tends to degenerate into the repetition of empty words with little thought of their meaning.

It is questionable whether our Lord's main objective was to provide His followers with a form of prayer to recite. That would be alien to the whole pattern of the Sermon. In the Prayer He lays down the principles governing man's relation to God, and these are relevant to Christians in every age. He did not say *In these precise words pray ye*', but '*After this manner pray ye*'. He gave a pattern, not an inflexible form. The exact words may vary greatly while the Prayer continues to conform to the pattern.

Before considering its petitions in detail, several points of interest about the Prayer deserve comment.

1. *It unfolds the relationships* the disciple sustains with the God to whom he prays

Father and child	—	'Our Father'
Deity and worshipper	—	'Hallowed be Thy name'
Sovereign and subject	—	'Thy Kingdom come'
Master and servant	—	'Thy will be done'
Benefactor and beneficiary	—	'Give us our daily bread'
Saviour and sinner	—	'Forgive us our trespasses'
Guide and pilgrim	—	'Lead us not into temptation'

In our prayers there can be a variety of approach to God as we consider Him at different times as sustaining a differing relationship with us. Today we may pray to Him especially as our Father, tomorrow as our mighty God, the next day as our King, then as our Saviour, etc.

2. *It defines the spirit* in which we should pray

An *unselfish* spirit	—	'Our'
A *filial* spirit	—	'Father'
A *reverent* spirit	—	'Hallowed be Thy name'
A *loyal* spirit	—	'Thy Kingdom come'
A *submissive* spirit	—	'Thy will be done'
A *dependent* spirit	—	'Give us our daily bread'
A *penitent* spirit	—	'Forgive us our trespasses'
A *humble* spirit	—	'Lead us not into temptation'
A *confident* spirit	—	'Thine is the Kingdom'

A *triumphant* spirit	—	'and the power'
An *exultant* spirit	—	'and the glory'

Here is a yardstick by which we can gauge whether our private prayers are acceptable to God. The spirit in which we pray is much more important than the words in which they are clothed.

3. *It reveals the priorities* to be observed in prayer. The striking thing is that the Prayer is halfway through before the petitioner's interests and needs are mentioned. This is the divine order, but not always the human practice. The heavenly has priority over the earthly. The first three petitions relate to God and His glory, the last three to man and his need.

4. *Marvel at its brevity*

This Prayer realises the Greek rhetorical ideal of an ocean of truth in a drop of speech. Only sixty-six words, yet what profundity! No 'holy loquacity' here, only six pointed petitions. Only God could compress so much meaning, and such a range of truth and instruction into so few words.

5. *Consider its comprehensiveness*

It is a model, a skeleton which contrives to embody in embryo every possible desire of the praying heart. It combines every divine promise and every human aspiration. It summarises all we should pray for. Nothing promised to the Christian is outside its scope.

6. *Think of its universality*

It covers all the needs that are common to humanity. It bears no mark of race or creed. People of every class and colour have made it the expression of their own hearts. It is the one religious formulary that is easily translatable into all languages.

7. *God is bound to answer every prayer after this pattern*

Can our petitions be brought within the scope of this Prayer? Then they are certain of answer, since its pattern is divinely given.

Now let us consider the Prayer in detail.

'Our Father who art in heaven'

In the place of prayer, selfishness is out. It is *our* Father', not *my* Father'. This is a prayer for the family of which God is the Father and we are members.

In what sense can we say that God is our Father? He is not the Cosmic Principle of Christian Science, nor the Universal Father of Modernism. Jesus spoke of two fatherhoods. To the Pharisees He said, 'Ye are of your father the devil' (John 8 : 44). This statement indicates that there is a rival kingdom to that of God—the kingdom of Satan. Those who have never entered the Kingdom of God through new birth, are still in the realm of Satan, and God is not their Father.

God is the Father only of those who have been born into His family. There is a limited sense in which He is the father of all men in a creatorial capacity, but that is not the sense here. As Head of the family, He knows what things we have need of before we ask Him (v. 8). He knows what is best and He does what is best.

The clause, 'who art in heaven', as someone has said, is not God's postal address. It indicates not so much His location as His elevation above man, His complete separation from earth's corruption. 'Our Father' awakens love in our hearts; 'Who art in heaven', engenders awe; and these two together constitute worship.

The first three petitions relate solely to God and this is fitting, since 'the chief end of man is to glorify God and to enjoy Him for ever'.

A Concern for His Name

'Hallowed be thy name'

God's name stands for His nature, His character, His Personality as revealed in Christ. The name of God is the eternally existing God Himself—the I AM. To hallow anything is to treat it as holy, to hold it in reverence.

This petition asks that He himself will be universally and perpetually honoured and reverenced among men and all created beings. He is to be given the unique place His name demands.

We are to cherish God's revelation of Himself, and to pray and work that it will be accepted by men everywhere. We who bear that name should have a loving concern for it, and should be deeply hurt when, instead of being reverenced, it is profaned and ignored.

A Concern for His Kingdom

'Thy Kingdom come'

Why do not all men hallow His name? Because they belong to the rival kingdom of Satan, and must first be brought into the Kingdom of God before they will reverence the King. The true disciple will have a yearning to see the sovereign reign of God in the hearts of men.

In the New Testament the Kingdom is represented as being both a present and a coming reality. 'Behold, the kingdom of God is within—or among—you' (Luke 17:21)—in the hearts of all who have given Him their allegiance. But in another sense it is still future, since no kingdom is fully established until the king is enthroned and all opposition subdued.

The loyal disciple has a passion for the spread of His sovereignty in the hearts of mankind here and now, but he also longs to see the Christ who is now rejected, enthroned and worshipped by all. He will therefore pray and work for the spread of the gospel and the overthrow of every opposing force, that the enthronement of Christ as Lord of all may be speedily consummated.

Actually the tense of the verb 'come' points to a climactic, not a gradual, coming of His Kingdom. This is, strictly speaking, a prayer for the second advent of Christ as King. In this petition the believer is saying, 'Even so, come, Lord Jesus.'

> O the joy to see Thee reigning,
> Thee my own beloved Lord!
> Every tongue Thy name confessing
> Worship, honour, glory, blessing
> Brought to Thee with one accord—
> Thee my Master and my Friend,
> Vindicated and enthroned
> Unto earth's remotest end
> Glorified, adored and owned!
>
> F. R. Havergal

A Concern for His Will

'Thy will be done on earth as it is done in heaven'

This logically follows the preceding petition. The believer cherishes a deep concern for the achieving of the purposes of God. He does not regard prayer as a means of getting his own will done, but as a means of getting God's will done in himself and in others.

> And shall I pray Thee to change Thy will, my Father –
> Until it be according unto mine?
> But no, Lord, no, that never shall be, rather
> I pray Thee blend my human will with Thine.

A. W. Carmichael

'Thy will be done' is not to be a cry of defeated resignation or an outlet for despair. The petition is not 'Thy will be borne, or suffered', but 'Thy will be *done*, as in heaven, so on earth.'

Sincerity demands that if we offer this petition, we are prepared for it to be done first of all in us. It admits of no reservations. The petition means, 'Enable us to obey thy revealed will as fully and as joyously as it is done by the angels in heaven.'

> Thou has sought God's will, but thine own was
>   sweet,
> Thou has sought God's will, thine was on the
>   throne,
> Now take thy will and lay it at His feet,
> And make His will thine own.

Author unknown

It is thought by many expositors that the phrase 'on earth as it is in heaven', refers back to each of these three petitions. If this is so, it would be most appropriate.

THE PETITIONS—CONCERNING MAN AND HIS NEEDS (VV. 11–13)

This section of the Prayer covers 'the essential needs of man, whether physical, mental or spiritual, and in the three spheres of time in which he moves'. Bread will meet his physical needs in the *present*. Forgiveness for sins in the *past* will meet his mental need, for nothing so disturbs the mind as unforgiven sin. Deliverance from the tempter's power anticipates his needs in the *future*.

Bread is provided by a loving *Father*. Forgiveness is dispensed by the *Son*. Deliverance and keeping from the power of the evil one are the prerogative of the *Holy Spirit*. Thus the three Persons of the Trinity unite to meet the physical mental and spiritual needs of the Christian, in the past, present and future. Oh, what a salvation this!

Dependence on God's Supply

'Give us this day our daily bread'

We are again reminded that we are not alone in our need, so 'my' becomes 'our'. We are to be concerned about our needy brother, and, where necessary, prayer should be followed by action. We should ask nothing for ourselves that we do not ask for others.

It is reasonable to think that 'daily bread' refers not only to the wheaten or barley loaf. Bread is referred to as 'the staff of life', a staple necessity. In this context it may well include whatever is necessary for the maintenance of daily life, in short, our temporal needs.

Until comparatively recently scholars were unable to arrive at the exact meaning of the word here translated 'daily'. Recent discoveries among the papyri resolved this problem. The word was found at the head of a woman's shopping list—'Goods for the coming day'.

So here the meaning is, 'Bread—the supply of our temporal needs—for the coming day'. If we offer the prayer in the morning, it covers the day already begun. If we offer it at night, it includes the following day.

The meaning is clear. We are to ask for God's provision *for the immediate future*. We are to live one day at a time, and for forty years the Israelites never missed a meal. So we are invited to ask daily for the supply of our temporal needs that lie just ahead, and our heavenly Father will not disappoint us.

Dependence on God's Mercy

'Forgive us our debts as we forgive our debtors'

The sense of unforgiven sin and guilt disturbs and creates turmoil in the mind, for there is a hunger of soul as well as a hunger of body. 'Canst thou not minister to a mind diseased?' was the entreaty of Macbeth to the physician who attended Lady Macbeth. We all need to come to our Father and ask His forgiveness.

'Debts', as in this petition, is a Jewish metaphor for sin, and is elsewhere so used by Jesus. A debt is an obligation incurred, in this case an obligation placed upon us by God which we have failed to discharge. It embraces sins of omission as well as sins of commission. Our sin has robbed both God and man of their due. We need forgiveness, and for this we are entirely dependent on God's mercy.

It may be asked, 'But if my sins were all forgiven when I came to the cross of Christ, why is there need to ask for forgiveness again?'

The answer is that we live in a polluted and defiling world. Although our sins have been forgiven in the judicial sense when we exercised faith in Christ for salvation, we do sin after conversion, and for these sins we need forgiveness.

Perhaps the distinction can be illustrated by referring to the two different aspects as (a) *judicial* forgiveness, granted by God as moral Governor of the universe, and as a result of this 'we are justified from all things',

Christ's atoning death for our sins has availed to remove our guilt, and the Law now has nothing against us; (b) *Paternal* forgiveness, bestowed by our Father on our confession of our sins.

Our Lord's words to Peter on the occasion of the foot-washing afford further elucidation. When Jesus would wash his feet Peter protested: 'Thou shalt never wash my feet.' Jesus answered, 'If I wash thee not, thou hast no part with me.' Peter saith to Him, 'Lord, not my feet only, but also my hands and my head.' Jesus saith to him: *'He that is washed'*—in the bath of regeneration —*'needeth not save to wash his feet, but is clean every whit'* (John 13:6-9). Jesus distinguishes between the bathing of the whole body and the washing of the feet —between regeneration and daily cleansing from the defilement contracted in this defiling world. For this we need constant cleansing, and it is this which is the issue here. It is not salvation, but unbroken fellowship within the family that is at stake. Sin always breaks fellowship and requires forgiveness.

This petition, 'Forgive us our debts as we have forgiven our debtors', sounds like a form of merit-theology, that we can earn forgiveness from God by forgiving others. But God's forgiveness is not a *quid pro quo*.

Jesus is here stating a principle in God's dealing with His children. He deals with us as we deal with others. He measures us by the yardstick we use on others. The prayer is not 'Forgive us *because* we forgive others', but 'Forgive us *even as* we have forgiven others'. Forgiveness is possible only when our wills have been brought back into conformity with the will of God, and if we have an unforgiving spirit, we are out of touch with God. The channel of God's forgiveness is blocked until we forgive our brother. How serious it would be for us to offer this petition if we have not forgiven others!

> 'Lead us not into temptation, but deliver us from
> the evil one'

The two elements in the petition belong to one another. It is a double-barrelled request. 'Evil' can equally
mean 'the evil one'. Evil is not an abstract principle. It
does not exist apart from personalities, and it focuses
in a malignant evil personage, the devil, from whose
power and subtlety we need deliverance.

The word 'temptation' is used in two senses in the
New Testament, one of which is neutral and the other
evil. It can mean either 'trial, testing', or 'enticement
to evil'. James assures us that God never incites to evil,
so in relation to God the word carries the first meaning
—trial or testing. God subjects His children to testing,
to eliminate the dross from the gold of their characters,
and to strengthen and establish them in holiness.
The devil tempts in order to induce them to fall into
sin.

The petition is therefore primarily a prayer for pro-
tection in time of testing and danger, when we are
open to the attacks of the evil one; and secondarily
it is a prayer for deliverance when enticed to sin by
him.

Our human nature shrinks from the fierce heat of the
testing crucible, and this is not sinful. Even the sinless
Christ shrank, as man, from the cup of suffering which
He was to drink, and the way in which He reacted
throws light on this very point. In the Garden of Geth-
semane His prayer was, 'O Father, if it be possible let
this cup pass from me, nevertheless, not as I will but
as thou wilt' (Matt. 26:39).

'Lead us not into temptation' voices the human
shrinking from testings which hold the possibility of
failing the test, and falling into sin. 'Deliver us from
the evil one' is a cry for deliverance in the hour of trial

Taken together, the double petition would mean, 'Father, spare me this trial, but if in thy wisdom thou dost see it to be necessary for thy glory and my spiritual development, give me the strength to come through it triumphantly, and unscathed in the conflict with the evil one.'

Missionary Application

This Prayer is not often regarded as having direct missionary overtones, and yet they are there clearly enough. The very fact of its universality makes it applicable to the missionary situation.

If we have *a concern for God's name*, and pray that it be hallowed, as in heaven, so on earth, surely it is to be hallowed everywhere and by everybody. But how can God's name be hallowed if it is not even known? One old pagan man who heard the gospel for the first time in his old age, and embraced it, said, 'If we had known, would we not have worshipped sooner?' There are still millions in like case, and if we have a concern for His name, we will do all in our power to see that it is made known to every creature.

If we have *a concern for God's Kingdom*, and yearn to see His sovereignty extended, we will be praying and working to that end. But how can His Kingdom come in the hearts of men, if they do not know that He is King, and so are unable to give Him their allegiance? And how will they learn this except through disciples like you and me? The Kingdom cannot come in its fullness until men know that He is King. Each soul won brings the Kingdom nearer.

If we have *a concern for His will*, and long that it be carried out on earth as it is in heaven, we will have an ambition to make it known by every means to all men, so that they may be obedient to it. How can men render obedience to God's will when they do not know what it is? And how shall they hear without a preacher? God's will is to bestow salvation on all who will receive it. *If*

His will was being done on earth by us who are His disciples, as it is done in heaven, there would be no unevangelised peoples in the world.

THE DOXOLOGY

'For Thine is the Kingdom, and the power and the glory, for ever, Amen.'

Although the doxology does not appear in the main manuscripts from which our New Testament is translated, it was used by the Church from very early times. Although apparently not a part of the Prayer as the Lord gave it, it is entirely in keeping with its spirit, and affords a fitting climax to *the Incomparable Prayer.*

9

The Simplicity of the Disciple's Possessions

Matthew 6 : 19–24

THE FORBIDDEN COVETOUSNESS

> Lay not up for yourselves treasures upon earth
> where moth and rust doth corrupt and where
> thieves break through and steal; but lay up for
> yourselves treasure in heaven, where neither moth
> nor rust doth corrupt, and where thieves do not
> break through nor steal: For where your treasure
> is, there will your heart be also (vv. 19 21).

In this section, Jesus contrasts the wordly disposition
with sane heavenly-mindedness. He emphasises what
He said on another occasion, though in different words,
'A man's life consisteth not in the abundance of the
things which he possesseth' (Luke 12 : 15). The disciple's
true treasure is in heaven, and he is preoccupied with
the things that are eternal. His primary motivation is
the glory of God, and his ambition, divine approval.

TREASURE ON EARTH

The key words of the passage occur in verse 19: 'for
yourselves'. Jesus does not say, as many wrongly read,

'Lay not up treasure on earth', a blanket command to save no money. The world's business would soon grind to a halt if this were the case. It would then be wrong to provide for old age, or to put aside for the education of one's children; but this would be in conflict with such passages as 2 Cor. 12:14 or 1 Tim. 5:8. The disciple is not to lay up treasure on earth *for himself*, hoarding money merely for his own indulgence and enjoyment.

In the Greek there is a play on words in this verse. Wycliff rendered it, 'Do not treasure to you treasures.' When our possessions become treasures to us, they possess us rather than we them, and we are on dangerous ground. The miser heaps up treasure on earth *for himself*, and all he achieves is to make himself miserable. The Christian philanthropist may lay up treasure on earth for use in the interests of the Kingdom and for the benefit of the needy. Because it is primarily for God and not for himself, his earthly treasure is transmuted into treasure in heaven.

To us treasure is that which we love most, which claims most of our thought and attention. Luther said in this connection, 'What a man loves, that is his god. For he carries it in his heart, he goes about with it night and day, he sleeps and wakes with it; be it what it may, wealth or pelf, pleasure or renown.'

'Where your treasure is, there will your heart be also.' Jesus was stating an obvious and indisputable fact. Treasures have an insidious way of captivating our hearts and drawing them away from God. Treasure always draws the heart after it. We are to store our wealth in heaven so that our hearts will be drawn upwards.

A merchant's interests lie where his investments are placed, and for this reason the disciple must avoid that which centres in this world only. If our hearts are seed-plots or culture-beds for the vices of avarice and covetousness, our whole life, even our faces, will be affected. It is not difficult to detect the face of a Scrooge. And who cannot recognise the face of a true saint? If we allow Christ to fill our hearts with His own magnanimity, we will not be able to conceal the radiance within.

The Christian is trustee, not owner, of his possessions. His responsibility is to administer them for God and his fellow men, not to hoard them. We are to share with others. Our storehouse is to be in heaven, not on earth.

The lesson cannot be mistaken. There is no permanence, no stability, no security in earthly treasure. Falling markets, stock exchange slumps, inflation, devaluation, and then the tax-man all erode and eat up treasure on earth, as Jesus went on to illustrate.

In the Orient wealth was preserved in three main forms—clothing, grain and gold.

Garments as a form of wealth, appear as an element in Achan's tragic sin : 'I saw among the spoils a goodly Babylonish garment . . . and I coveted it . . . and I took it' (Josh. 7:21).

Grain as a form of wealth, appears in the parable of the rich fool, whose crops were so abundant that he said, 'I will pull down my barns and build greater' (Luke 12:15).

Gold or precious stones as a form of wealth are exemplified in the parable of 'the treasure hid in a field' (Matt. 13:44). In the Palestine of those days, there were no banks in which people could deposit their money. They therefore resorted to concealing it in their houses, or burying it in a field.

Jesus, realistic as ever, and talking in terms familiar to His hearers, pointed out that treasure on earth was very vulnerable and precarious. Clothing is subject to the ravages of the moth. Grain can be consumed by rats and mice. Gold and jewels can be stolen by thieves.

'Rust' in verse 20 is perhaps not the best translation, and certainly not the only translation of the Greek word used. It means 'something that gnaws, or eats or corrodes'. Nowhere else in the New Testament is it translated 'rust'. As food is one of the main forms of stored wealth in the East, the word would perhaps be better translated by giving its more customary meaning of 'eating'. Rats and mice can gnaw and eat away the wealth of the farmer.

It is interesting that the Greeks termed burglars 'mud-diggers'. The allusion is to the practice of the burglar digging his way through the mud wall of an Eastern home to steal the concealed treasure.

In view of all these factors, Jesus issued a direction to His disciples, and incidentally to us; 'Do not *continue the habit of laying up* for yourselves treasure on earth', for that is the significance of the tense of the verb. If you are doing this, stop it!

Sound reasons lie behind His exhortation. (a) Earthly treasures will perish, and in any case, these forms of wealth are not currency in heaven. There, gold is used for road-metal. (b) Death is inevitable, and there are no pockets in a shroud. (c) Devotion to the task of accumulating wealth for oneself automatically erodes devotion to God. (d) In the long run, treasure tends to become master, not servant.

TREASURE IN HEAVEN

Wealth transmuted into heavenly treasure is imperishable. No natural process of erosion or corruption can affect it. Peter describes our heavenly inheritance in a series of striking words in 1 Pet. 1 : 4.

As to its substance, it is *incorruptible*, beyond the reach of death or decay. It is indestructible, unaffected by moths and rats and thieves. As to its purity, it is *undefiled*, stainless, untarnishable, unpolluted. The word is derived from a precious stone to which nothing would adhere. Filth automatically fell away from it. As to its charm, it is *unfading*, unwithering, preserving its freshness and fragrance even in a foetid atmosphere. What a refreshing contrast with the transience and impermanence of treasure on earth!

It is God's desire that we go to a heaven richly furnished with the materials we have sent on ahead of us. This conception is not peculiar to Christianity, for the Koran has this sentence: 'When a man dies, men ask how much he left behind, whereas the angels ask how much he has sent before him.'

Laying up Treasure in Heaven

How may we lay up treasure in heaven? How send on before us that which can be converted into heavenly treasure? Bishop Gore says we can answer this question with great assurance:

> To lay up treasure in heaven, is to do acts which promote, or belong to the Kingdom of God; and what our Lord assures us is that any act of our hands, any thought of our hearts, any word of our lips which promotes the Kingdom—all such activity, though it may seem for the moment to be lost, is really stored up for us in the divine treasure-house.[1]

It is gloriously true that there is a divine alchemy that can transmute the lead of earth into the gold of heaven. Golden sovereigns can be changed into redeemed souls. Things done primarily for the glory of God and secondarily for the welfare of mankind, constitute treasure in heaven. Our acts of devotion and service here, become our treasure there. Acts of kindness and mercy performed, elements of character painfully inwrought, money given for the salvation of souls, all form part of our heavenly capital.

Nowadays when capital is so ruthlessly pruned by taxation and inflation, some wise Christians have forestalled the erosion of their wealth and the corresponding limitation of their ability to give, by constituting evangelical trust or foundations. Through these agencies, a great deal of taxation is legally obviated, and God's work can be supported in perpetuity. By thus refusing to lay up treasure for themselves, not only do they accumulate treasure in heaven but lend invaluable help to the vastly important tasks of evangelism and missions.

Origen has recorded a reputed saying of Jesus: 'Prove yourselves good money-changers'. If this is an authentic saying, its meaning is not difficult to discern. We are to employ some medium of exchange, whereby our service and stewardship on earth can become heavenly currency.

> *Riches I heed not, nor man's empty praise;*
> *Thou mine inheritance, now and always:*
> *Thou and Thou only, first in my heart,*
> *High King of heaven, my treasure Thou art*
>
> M. E. Byrne

SINGLE VISION

> The light of the body is the eye: if therefore thine eye be single, thy whole body shall be full of light. But if thine eye be evil, thy whole body shall be full of darkness. If therefore the light that is in thee be darkness, how great is that darkness (vv. 22–3).

Preoccupation with amassing treasure darkens the mind as well as captures the heart (v. 21). 'Light' in verse 22a should be 'lamp', for the eye is only the light-receiver, the window that enables one to see clearly. The condition of the soul's eye determines the way we look at things. If the eye is 'single', we look at things one way, but if it is 'evil', in quite another.

When used in the *physical* sense, 'single' means 'healthy, clear', and 'evil', 'unhealthy, out of order'. If used in the *ethical* sense, the one means 'pure', and the other 'covetous or avaricious'. William Barclay points

122

out that 'single' is used of generosity, and 'evil' for the opposite, a concept which would fit this context well.

The disciple whose soul's eye is healthy, without astigmatism, sees things clearly and in correct proportion. But if his eyes are astigmatic, things are out of focus, and his faulty vision will result in wrong action. Instead of laying up treasure in heaven, the one whose eye is unhealthy suffers from spiritual double vision. He wants to have his treasure on earth and in heaven too. Through having one eye on earth's rewards and the other on heaven's, he develops a spiritual squint.

Although we have two eyes, if they are healthy, there is only one focal point; but astigmatic eyes give a distorted vision. If normal spiritual vision is to be restored, there must be adjustment to God's will. If our eyes are focused on Christ, He will fill our lives with heaven's light. But if we persist in the pursuit of the material to the exclusion of the spiritual, how intense is the resulting darkness! The deterioration of God's best becomes the devil's worst.

SINGLE SERVICE

> No man can serve two masters: for either he will hate the one and love the other, or else he will hold to the one and despise the other. Ye cannot serve God and mammon (v. 24).

One result of this double vision is the attempt to serve two masters, God and mammon. In these days of multiple employment it is possible to serve two masters, with complete loyalty to both, but it was not possible for those envisaged in Jesus's figure. The more correct translation would be 'You cannot *be slave* to two masters', and a slave is one who has no rights over himself at all. He is utterly and for ever at the disposal of his one master.

Life is so constituted that man has no choice about

serving, but he can choose whom or what he serves. He can serve either God or mammon, but not both at the same time. He cannot be slave both to God and to material things.

'Mammon' on the lips of Jesus meant 'property, earthly goods', but with a derogatory sense of the materialistic, anti-godly, sinful. In the earthly property which a man gathers, in which he erroneously seeks security, and to which he gives his heart, Jesus finds the very opposite of God. Because of the demonic power immanent in possessions, surrender to them brings practical enslavement.[2] So mammon does not mean wealth *per se*, but wealth become an idol.

The insidious effect of money on character is so well known as to need no amplification. It demands a man's whole attention, and that inevitably means a divided loyalty, for God demands the whole devotion too. We are to worship Him with all our heart. He must be Lord of all or He is not Lord at all. 'Ye *cannot*'—not *must not*—'serve God and mammon.' It cannot be done. If we attempt to serve both, we will love one and hate—love less—the other. If two masters claimed a slave's service, he was bound to reject one, for he could render total obedience to only one.

Money is neutral; there is nothing inherently evil in it. How it is gained, how it is regarded and how it is used—these are the things which determine whether it is mammon or heavenly treasure. Jesus did not condemn the rich young man simply because he was rich. The reason 'he went away sorrowful' was that his great possessions had become a great idol. He did not possess them, they possessed him. When faced with the real issue, he rejected the service of God and chose mammon. His sin was that he laid up treasure on earth *for himself*.

The Christian man of business constantly faces a choice between God and mammon. Often he must choose between profit and principle. A large profit at the cost of a little principle is often the devil's lure. Preacher and missionary are not exempt from this tension, but their ministry must never be influenced by financial considerations. The pursuit of mammon will unfit them for their Master's service.

The best way of breaking the power of the material over our lives, is to devote it to spiritual ends. It was this Jesus advocated: 'Make friends for yourselves by means of the mammon of unrighteousness; that when it fails, they may receive you into the eternal dwellings' (Luke 16:9 N.A.S.V.). If we devote our possessions to the spread of the gospel and the winning of souls, we will not go to a lonely heaven. There will be those on the other side waiting to welcome us, who have found their way there because we resisted the lure of mammon, and instead of laying up treasure on earth, exchanged it for heavenly treasure.

1. Gore, *The Sermon on the Mount*, p. 143.
2. See Kittell, *Theological Dictionary of the New Testament* (Grand Rapids, Eerdmans, 1967), vol, iv, p. 389.

10

The Serenity of the Disciple's Trust

Matthew 6 : 25–34

THE FORBIDDEN WORRY

> For this reason I say unto you, do not be anxious for your life, as to what you shall eat, or what you shall drink; nor for your body, as to what you shall put on. Is not life more than food, and the body than clothing? (v. 25 N.A.S.V.).

If mammon tends to be the characteristic temptation of men, perhaps worry is the special besetment of women—although at times the lines may cross! It is a temptation of the rich as well as the poor. The rich man worries over what he has, the poor man over what he hasn't. It assails the young as well as the old. The schoolboy worries about his examinations and what he will do when he leaves school. The elderly worry about the imponderables of old age. For such a universal problem, it is not surprising that the Lord had sage counsel to give.

We would miss the point of this section if we did not understand the clause translated 'take no thought' in the Authorised Version. The expression signifies a concern for the means of life which has degenerated into anxiety, that is, *anxious care*, or worry.

Jesus does not denounce the prudent forethought that is essential to a well-ordered life. Nor does He advocate careless improvidence. It is not concern, but over-concern, such as that exhibited by Martha, that He forbids. The antithesis of anxious thought is not carelessness, or even carefreeness, but confidence and trust in a Father's love and care. From this the devil seeks to seduce us into the fruitless and debilitating sin of worry. If he fails with the bait of avarice, he will try the snare of worry.

Once again the tense of the verbs is significant. In verse 25 the meaning is, 'Stop worrying!' If the habit already has you in its grip, stop it! In verse 31 the meaning is, 'don't worry', or 'never worry'. If worry is not yet habitual, don't let it grip you. No matter what happens, don't worry. Since Christ commands this, then in the Spirit's power it must be a possible goal.

To support His exhortation, Jesus selected three areas of life which are major matters of concern to all—eating, drinking, clothing. He illustrated His teaching by three parables from Nature.

It should not be supposed that by His selection of these three activities Jesus gave tacit liberty to worry about other things than those He mentioned. He was enunciating a general principle, the nub of which is that we are not to worry about anything, however important and essential it may seem. Worry is not something in which we are to be selective, but something to be totally abjured.

Food and drink and clothing often caused deep concern to the Palestinian people. Jesus's counsel was therefore especially relevant to His audience. Then as now in the East, as the time for the new harvest drew near, the grain stored from the last harvest often ran low, and the number of meals had to be reduced to eke out the supply. Naturally, food became a worrying preoccupation.

In the burning summer heat streams dried up and

water was frequently in short supply. To the poorer people—and it is to them that the words are primarily addressed—an annual change of clothing was by no means automatic, and clothing a family could be a worrying affair. So the Preacher reinforced His counsel with homely logic, and shows that restless anxiety springs from lack of quiet trust in God.

WORRY IS NEEDLESS

> Look at the birds of the air, that they do not sow, neither do they reap, nor gather into barns; and yet *your heavenly Father feeds them*. Are you not worth much more than they? (v. 26 N.A.S.V.).

Jesus appeals to the evidence of His Father's providential and parental care, as a ground for abandoning worry about their temporal or other concerns. The Father's care of the lower creation is an argument for His provision for the higher creation. Birds cannot store up food or drink for future needs, and yet their needs are supplied. In any case, worrying would not improve the situation if food and drink were in short supply. Worry is needless with such a heavenly Father.

WORRY IS FUTILE

> And which of you by being anxious *can add a single cubit to his life's span*? And why are you anxious about clothing? Observe how the lilies of the field grow; they do not toil, nor do they spin. Yet I say to you that even Solomon in all his glory did not clothe himself like one of these (vv. 27–9 N.A.S.V.).

It is generally agreed that 'stature' in the Authorised Version would be better rendered 'span of life'. On the meaning of the word, Schneider writes: 'The context demands that *helikia* should mean "span of life" . . . Jesus is saying that anxious care is futile. No one thereby can add one fraction of time to his life.'[1] Indeed, worry is more likely to shorten life than to lengthen it. We achieve ridiculously little by our worrying, and more often than not it proves futile because the tomorrow we worry about frequently never comes.

Worry is futile because it cannot recall the *past*. It has gone beyond recall. Nor can worry avert disaster or evade the difficulties that loom in the *future*, so anxiety about the future is futile. Worry about *present* crises and problems is more likely to produce ulcers and thrombosis than solutions. It only serves to impair our judgment, and renders us less competent to make sound decisions or meet the emergency.

All of your care—the yesterdays long vanished,
The vain regrets, the heartbreak, and the tears,
Wrong choices made, hopes unfulfilled and
  broken
The blighted harvest of the locust years,
Leave it with Him, He knows the load you bear
For you are His, and you are in His care.

All of your care—tomorrow with its problems,
The lengthening shadows of the passing days,
The secret fears, of failure, weakness, suffering
Of grief and loss, and straitened lonely ways,
Leave it with Him, your future He will share
For you are His, the object of His care.

All of your care—today with all its burdens,
Temptations sore, and trials the long hours
  through,
Though faith be faltering, and the conflict
  endless
Yet He is watching and concerned for you,
Lay at His feet each burden that you bear,
Leave them with Him, because you are His
  care.

Joan Suisted

129

'Consider how the wild flowers grow,' Jesus challenged them. With what gorgeous colours your Father paints them. See how effortlessly they thrive under His providential care. If He does that for a wild flower, what will He do for His own children? Then why worry? Worry is futile.

WORRY IS FAITHLESS

> But if God so arrays the grass of the field which is alive today and tomorrow is thrown into the furnace, will He not much more do so for you, *O men of little faith?* Do not be anxious then, saying, what shall we eat? or what shall we drink? or with what shall we clothe ourselves? (vv. 30–1 N.A.S.V.).

We are apt to shrug off the worry habit as some amiable hereditary weakness that we must learn to live with. But Jesus did not so view it. To Him it was a sinful lack of faith in His Father. He described worriers as 'men of little faith', and this is no amiable weakness, for 'without faith it is impossible to please God'.

The author once hung in his office a motto that never failed to draw comment. It ran: WHY TRUST WHEN YOU CAN WORRY?

Almost invariably visitors would comment that the words were wrong way round—and so they were. But their reversal served to draw attention to the fact that very many Christians are more prone to worry faithlessly about their problems, than to trust God to solve them. We trust God for the stupendously important matter of our salvation, and then are strangely timid about trusting Him for our other infinitely less important concerns.

Trust and worry cannot sleep in the same bed. They are mutually antagonistic. The one negates the other. Worry is faithless.

For all these things the Gentiles (heathen) eagerly seek; for your heavenly Father knows that you need all these things (v. 32 N.A.S.V.).

By worrying we become like the heathen, who are absorbed in the pursuit of earthly things. Thus we lose our distinctive character as the salt of the earth. We worry about the same things as those who have no revelation of God as a loving heavenly Father. Anxiety is unfilial as well as unbelieving. It is the heathen's fatalistic belief that the happenings of life are either inevitable or accidental; therefore, they say, 'Let us eat, drink, and be merry for tomorrow we die.' Worry is pagan.

FAITH'S PRIORITY

Faith persistently rejects anxious care, and will not allow it standing room. As fast as the tendency to worry asserts itself, it is for us to meet it with the affirmation of faith in the love and care of God. If we trust, we will not worry, and if we worry, we are not trusting. Worry is not a characteristic of one who really knows his heavenly Father, who is so utterly trustworthy.

Tucked away in this delightful and colourful homily on anxious care, is one of the key principles, not only of the Sermon, but of the whole Christian life.

Seek first His Kingdom and His righteousness, and all these things will be added to you (v. 33 N.A.S.V.).

If we accord priority to the interests of the Kingdom of God and the attainment of holy character, we need have no anxiety. Once we get our priorities right, everything else will fall into place. The Father will supply everything really necessary.

This verse is to be taken at face value, and acted upon accordingly. If we make God's triumph our concern, He will make all that affects us His concern, and anxiety will be totally unnecessary.

Trust in the heavenly Father's care will result in tranquillity and serenity. This does not mean that faith will not be tested, but it will be able to surmount the severest test.

In His closing exhortation, our Lord clinched all He had been saying about the sin of worry :

> Therefore, do not be anxious for tomorrow; for tomorrow will care for itself (v. 34 N.A.S.V.).

Why add tomorrow's possible anxieties to the very real ones of today? Why go out to meet the unknown future? for that is what worry does. Each day will bring its own quota of care, so why increase today's load by ante-dating tomorrow's troubles? All that will achieve, will be to unfit you to meet the exigencies of tomorrow.

> Why, therefore, should we do ourselves the
>   wrong,
> Or others—that we are not always strong,
> That we are ever overborne with care,
> That we should ever weak and heartless be,
> Anxious or troubled, when with us is
>   prayer,
> And joy and strength and courage are with
>   Thee?
>
> R. C. Trench

1. See Kittell, *Theological Dictionary of the New Testament*, vol. 11, p. 942).

11

The Sanity of the Disciple's Judgment

Matthew 7 : 1–12

THE FORBIDDEN CRITICISM

In this section Jesus deals with the critical spirit. He draws attention to three forms which it may take, and three related laws. Criticism may be destructive, deluded or discerning.

DESTRUCTIVE CRITICISM

> Judge not, that ye be not judged. For with what judgment ye judge, ye shall be judged; and with what measure ye mete, it shall be measured to you again (v. 1).

The word 'judge' carries with it the idea of censoriousness, or carping criticism. In its strict sense, it means simply 'to discriminate' or 'to distinguish', and does not necessarily have a bad connotation. Our 'judging' could as easily issue in commendation as condemnation. We are not to be undiscriminating, but we are to be uncritical, for taken in its context the word refers to censorious, sharp, unjust criticism. We are to judge, but not to prejudge, i.e. to be prejudiced.

In the course of normal living it is necessary for us constantly to exercise our God-given critical faculty, and make our own assessment of facts and people. But it is the purpose for which we make our judgment, and the way in which we express and use it that determine its moral quality and effects. It can be bane or blessing according to the spirit in which it is uttered. We are not to be credulously blind to moral evil and failure in others, but neither are we to cherish a censorious spirit or indulge in critical talk about them. Such criticism is always flattering to ourselves, for it is always delivered from a position of superiority.

Destructive criticism is no Christian employment, and Jesus said it must be decisively and permanently abandoned. The tense of the verb indicates that Jesus was warning against a practice His hearers were already indulging. He gave a command that may very well be applicable to us all—'Stop criticising!' Paul gives the same authoritative and absolute injunction: 'Let us not therefore judge one another any more' (Rom. 14:13).

There are valid reasons for this command of Christ. At best our knowledge of the circumstances can be only partial. We do not know all the background. We see the issue, but not all the factors involved. We see the flaws and failures, but who can accurately assess the influence of heredity or environment on the failure? We see the fall before the temptation, but who can measure its intensity, or the hidden resistance that preceded it?

> Who made the heart, 'tis He alone
>   Decidedly can try us.
> He knows each chord, its various tone,
>   Each spring, its various bias;
> Then at the balance, let's be mute,
>   We never can adjust it,
> What's done we partly may compute,
>   But know not what's resisted.
>
> Robert Burns

134

We form our judgments from superficial data gleaned from outward appearance. Only God knows all the facts, and therefore only God can reach a correct judgment. 'If we knew all, our criticism might well have turned to admiration.'

There is sound wisdom in the legal maxim, that an *ex parte* statement should never be accepted without challenge. There is always another side to every story. It would be going much too far to accept the French proverb, 'To know all is to forgive all', but there is more than a grain of truth in it. If we possessed more complete knowledge, we would indulge in less unloving criticism.

Then, too, our judgment is fallible. Even if we did know all the facts, would we necessarily interpret them correctly? Two people, faced with the same set of facts, may arrive at diametrically opposite conclusions. This frequently happens when a jury brings in a divided finding. They all listened to the same submissions and arguments, but formed different conclusions. It is not for us to usurp the judge's role and pass the final verdict.

> *Judge not; the workings of his brain*
> *And of his heart thou cannot see.*
> *What looks to thy dim eyes a stain*
> *In God's pure light may only be*
> *A scar brought from some well-won field*
> *Where thou wouldst only faint and yield.*
>
> Author unknown

In the course of their administrative duties, Christian leaders have to discriminate and make decisions in the light of the facts as they have them, and of their best judgment. But the foregoing factors should be kept in mind, and dependence on God for heavenly wisdom should be the prevailing attitude in so delicate an operation.

> In the way you judge you will be judged; and by
> your standard of measure it shall be measured
> to you (V. 2 N.A.S.V.).

Jesus draws His hearers' attention to the law of cause
and effect, of action and reaction. Harrington C. Lees[1]
points out that Jesus looks back to the three principles
with which he dealt in the last section in regard to the
actions of the heart and of the mind and of the eye, and
states the three laws which must be borne in mind, if a
wise equilibrium is to be preserved. The law of retribution is the first of these.

Censorious criticism is a boomerang that rebounds
on the one who throws it. The echo returns the exact
words that are spoken. Our unloving criticism will re-
coil on our own heads. The measure we employ for
gauging the faults of others, will be the measure used
on our conduct by both God and man. 'Thou wicked
servant, out of thine own mouth will I judge thee,' is
the principle.

Scripture is replete with illustrations of this law. With
poetic justice the wicked Haman swung on the very
gallows he had erected for Mordecai. When Adoni-bezek
was captured and punished by the Israelites, he said,
'Seventy kings with their thumbs and great toes cut off
used to pick up scraps at my table; as I have done, so
God hath requited me' (Judges 1 : 7).

There is another, though less important reason why
we should stop criticising. Nothing will make our company less welcome to right-thinking people. Greek
mythology had its god Momus, the god of criticism, who
lived with the other gods on Mount Olympus. No
matter how loud the other gods were in their praise,
Momus always found something to criticise in the subject of their discussion. On one occasion, Jupiter,
Minerva and Neptune had a competition to see who

could make the most perfect object. Jupiter made a man, Minerva a house and Neptune a bull. When the gods were invited to pass judgment, Momus found fault with all three; with the man, because he had no window in his breast, through which the thoughts of his soul might be read; with the house because it was not on wheels so that it could be removed from bad neighbours; with the bull, because its horns were not below its eyes, so that he might see when he butted with them. Captious criticism, do you say? Much of the criticism current in Christian circles is no better based. Is it to be wondered at that Momus became so unpopular on Mount Olympus that the gods banished him from their company?

DELUDED CRITICISM

> And why do you look at the speck in your brother's eye, but do not notice the log that is in your own eye? Or how can you say to your brother, let me take the speck out of your eye, and behold the log is in your own eye? You hypocrite, first take the log out of your own eye, and then you will see clearly enough to take the speck out of your brother's eye (vv. 3–5 N.A.S.V.).

With clear perception Jesus laid bare the insincerity of a great deal of the criticism people indulge in. Those who are lynx-eyed in detecting minute defects in the character of others are usually incredibly blind to their own glaring faults. A passion to put others right and make them over may very well be suspect in the light of these words of the Master. As someone has said, 'a blind guide is bad enough, but a blind optician is a still more ridiculous anomaly.' Our criticism is so often wrong because our moral vision is blurred by our own faults.

Were it not so true to life, the illustration of the log large enough to make a rafter; and the tiny speck of sawdust, would be ludicrous; but Jesus employed the figure of hyperbole to make His audience conscious of the extent of their guilt of this very sin. So often we have in our own characters a larger edition of the very defect we see and criticise in others.

The jealous person is the most apt to detect jealousy in others, because that is the way he would react were he in the same circumstances. The merciless critic has no right to condemn others while oblivious of his own shortcomings. His need is self-criticism.

The point of the illustration is that the Lord desires the removal of both the speck and the log. His concern is for both men. But before we are qualified to engage in the delicate task of removing the speck from our brother's eye, we must first deal with the log in our own. Otherwise, our judgment is bound to be prejudiced. It is often the case that the man who is guilty of large frauds in business, is the most severe on petty theft among his employees.

The Law of Restraint

Before we criticise our fellow Christian, we should engage in healthy self-criticism, lest it be said of us, 'Therefore thou art inexcusable, O man, whosoever thou art that judgest, for wherein thou judgest another, thou condemnest thyself; for thou that judgest doeth the same things' (Rom. 2 : 1). Honest self-criticism will restrain from harsh criticism of others. And this same self-criticism will save us from the judgment of God, for 'if we would judge ourselves, we would not be judged' (1 Cor. 11 : 31).

'Praying Hyde' of India learned a lesson which he said was the most salutary and educative the Lord had ever taught him. He was deeply burdened about the spiritual condition of a certain Indian pastor, and not without cause. He resolved to spend some time interceding for him.

He began pouring out his heart to God somewhat as

follows: 'Oh God, Thou knowest that brother, how . . .' 'cold', he was going to say, when suddenly a hand seemed to be laid on his lips, and a voice said to him in stern reproach, 'He that toucheth him, toucheth the apple of mine eye.'

A great horror came over him. He had been guilty before God of 'accusing the brethren'. He had been judging his brother. He felt rebuked and humbled before God. It was he himself who first needed putting right. He confessed this sin and claimed forgiveness and cleansing. Then he prayed, 'Father, show me what things are lovely and of good report in my brother's life.'

Like a flash he remembered how that man had given up all for Christ, enduring much suffering from his relatives. He was reminded of years of hard work, of the tact with which he managed a difficult congregation, of the many quarrels he had healed, of what a model husband he was. All his prayer season was spent in praise for his brother instead of prayer.

Mark the result on the pastor's life. When Hyde went down to the plains, he found that just at the time of his humbling experience, the pastor had received a great spiritual uplift. While Hyde was praising, God was blessing.[2]

Here is another important spiritual principle. Our prayers for others must not degenerate into an oblique criticism, as they sometimes do. 'Get the beam out of your own eye,' said Campbell Morgan, 'get the ungodly and unchristlike endeavour to find the mote destroyed; and then you will see clearly, not the mote, but how to remove it.'

DISCERNING CRITICISM

> Do not give what is holy to dogs, and do not throw your pearls before swine, lest they trample them under their feet, and turn and tear you to pieces (v. 6 N.A.S.V.).

The same Lord who said, 'Judge not', also said, 'Judge righteous judgment' (John 7:24). In saying this, Jesus did not contradict himself for there is a permissible and necessary criticism as well as a forbidden one. We must discriminate between people, and act in the light of our appraisal.

Christ uses the terms 'dogs' and 'swine', not offensively, but as typical of certain classes of people—obviously unholy people.

In the Orient the dogs were often repulsive and foul scavengers. Jesus probably had in mind the gorging of a filthy dog on the sacred flesh of the holy burnt-offering. The sacred character of the food meant nothing to the dog.

Swine were unclean animals to the Jew, and eating their flesh was an abomination. These two animals are mentioned together again, and in a similar context: 'The dog is turned to his own vomit, and the sow to her wallowing in the mire' (2 Pet. 2:22). The terms are obviously used here of those who are not Christians, for Christians are described as 'sheep'.

The priests must not throw that part of the holy sacrifice reserved for them, to the filthy dogs. Pearls are not to be thrown to unappreciative swine who might mistake them for beans, or barley. Finding themselves cheated, they might trample the pearls underfoot, and turn and rend the deceiver.

The figure teaches that spiritual treasures are not to be given to those who have no appreciation of them. While we are not to be censoriously critical, we must exercise discernment and discrimination in our dealings with men. The materialist has little appreciation for the spiritual, because it is understood only by the spiritual man. All truth is not appropriate for all persons, and we need spiritual insight to discern what is right for them.

Before sharing the deep things of our own inner experience, we should appraise those with whom we propose to share it. Even our Lord shared truth with His disciples only 'as they were able to bear it' (Mark 4:35). All truth is not appropriate for every occasion.

While we must avoid judging our fellows lightly or hastily, when a man has displayed his true character, we should be careful what we say to him. This counsel from our Lord authorises us to exercise a sensible and discerning criticism; and this power divinely illumined will enable us to know what is fitting for those to whom we speak, and what is the correct occasion.

The Law of Reticence

Jesus practised His own precepts. When He was brought before Herod, the King 'was exceeding glad, and questioned Him with many words: but he answered him nothing'. He refused to give what was holy to dogs or to cast His pearls before swine. He refused to gratify Herod's vain curiosity. It is for us to follow His example in observing the law of reticence.

Is there a panacea for the critical spirit? This passage gives an answer. Exercise restraint and reticence in criticising others, for it is retributive. 'Each of us, then, will have to answer for himself to God. So let us stop criticising' (Rom. 4:12, 13 Moffatt).

IMPORTUNITY IN PRAYER

> Ask and it shall be given you; seek and ye shall find; knock and it shall be opened unto you: for every one that asketh receiveth; and he that seeketh findeth; and to him that knocketh, it shall be opened (vv. 7, 8).

The connection between this homily on prayer and what precedes it is not immediately obvious. Those who consider the Sermon to be a collection of the sayings of Jesus and not a connected discourse, would concur with one of their number who wrote: 'This passage on prayer stands in no topical relation with its context. In

Luke it fittingly follows the Lord's Prayer and the parable of the Friend at Midnight'[3]

But is this necessarily so? Is there no connection? If we follow the general principle of interpretation, and take this paragraph in its preceding and succeeding context, we will discover a connection that is by no means strained or unnatural.

Jesus has been discussing with His disciples what has been called 'the Number-One sin of the Christian'—criticism. He illustrated His point by the hyperbole of the speck and the log, emphasising the delicacy of the task of removing the speck from the brother's eye. He stressed the necessity of discriminating between man and man, and truth and truth, for Church history bears tragic record of the havoc wrought in the Church through failure to discern wolves in sheep's clothing.

A consideration of what is involved in observing these duties compels one to join Paul in his exclamation, 'Who is sufficient for these things?' It is far too delicate and complicated a task for unaided human wisdom and tact. How can we be sure we are judging righteous judgment?

Then, too, Jesus immediately followed these encouragements to prayer with the Golden Rule, which makes such stupendous demands on Christian love. How can we rise to this exalted standard? He anticipates the problem and gives the answer—Ask, seek, knock. 'If any man lack wisdom, let him *ask* of God . . .'

This would seem to be the reason why Jesus reverted to a subject already treated—it is the only time He does so—and added to the element of trust in prayer the dimension of importunity.

So when we face the delicate task of acting as spiritual optician to remove the speck from our brother's eye, we will ask for heavenly wisdom first to discern and remove any log in our own eye, so that we can see clearly how to help our brother.

And when we are confronted with the necessity of

distinguishing between a brother and a 'dog'—an unworthy person—when we have to discern what truths of Scripture are apppropriate to different persons or groups, we will be importunate in seeking divine aid and discrimination.

If this is the correct interpretation, then the context afforded the Lord the occasion for enunciating another great and general principle in the realm of prayer.

There is an ascending scale of intensity in this threefold exhortation and assurance. We are given strong encouragement to press our suit with great importunity. The promise of answer is six times repeated.

Ask is so simple a word that a child understands it. It is to make a petition for something we desire or need. The one who asks makes no contribution to the answer. *Seek* goes further, and implies participation. The verbal request is followed up by action. For example it would be futile to ask God for a deeper knowledge of Scripture if we did not seek the truth by diligent study. Asking alone would be insufficient.

Knocking imports yet another element—importunity and persistence. The tense of the verbs indicates a repeated action, knocking and keeping on knocking, seeking and keeping on seeking, asking and keeping on asking. We are to persevere and refuse to be discouraged. This thought is amplified in the parable of the importunate widow whose persistence gained her the answer. Such an attitude pleases God, for it proves our sincerity and strength of purpose. Prayer is not the act of a moment but the maintained attitude of the heart.

> Or what man is there of you, whom if his son asks bread, will he give him a stone? Or if he ask a fish, will he give him a serpent? If ye then being evil know how to give good gifts to your children, how much more shall your Father which is in heaven give good things to them that ask him (vv. 9–11).

It is to be noted that the things to which Jesus refers in this section—bread, fish, and, Luke adds, an egg—were not luxuries, but the staple diet, the basic necessities of life for those to whom He spoke. He deliberately by-passed luxuries and used the basic essentials to illustrate His Father's impartial love and provision for His children, in order to encourage His disciples to ask and seek and knock until they received an answer. They can be confident that their heavenly Father will give them all necessary things, all good things and no bad things. This is brought out in the three contrasting things mentioned. Bread and a stone are the best and worst things to give to a hungry person, fish and a serpent are the ceremonially clean and unclean, and an egg and a scorpion have the germ of life and the 'virus of death' in them.

In drawing a parallel between His Father and an earthly father, Jesus also made a distinction. 'If ye then, being evil . . .' This statement demolishes any idea of God being a universal Father of regenerate and ungenerate alike. He made it clear that in each of us there is an element of evil that makes regeneration a necessity.

Monica was deeply burdened for the salvation of her profligate son, Augustine. When she heard of his plan to go to Italy, she prayed earnestly that he might not go, lest it prove his ruin. To her, this was the 'good thing' she most desired. But despite her prayers, he went—and found Christ there! Our heavenly Father knows which are the 'good things', and will answer our heart's desire.

In the parallel passage in Luke 11 : 13, 'good things' is replaced by 'the Holy Spirit'. Since the good things in this passage are the very necessities of life, the implication is that the Holy Spirit is not an optional extra for especially pious people, a luxury that can be done without, but is One who is absolutely indispensable to even minimum Christian living. This should make any who avoid teaching on the Holy Spirit because some have gone to excess, think again. Further reference to this important verse will be made in the last chapter.

THE GOLDEN PRINCIPLE

> Therefore all things whatsoever ye would that men should do to you, do ye even so to them: for this is the law and the prophets (v. 12).

In this saying the Sermon reaches its apex. It is a summary of the law concerning man's relation to man. It is the full expression of our social responsibility, the principle of all social conduct.

It is often rightly affirmed that other great men enunciated this principle before Christ, and that there was nothing new in it. It is quite true that others have advocated a similar truth, such men as Socrates, Aristotle, Confucius and Hillel, but there is a significant difference. 'So expressed as it is here—in immediate connection with, and as the sum of such duties as has just been enjoined, and such principles as had been before taught —it is to be found nowhere else. And the best commentary on this fact is, that never till our Lord came down thus to teach, did men effectually and widely exemplify it in their practice.'[5]

Between our Lord's teaching on the social duties of man and that of the others mentioned, there is a crucial difference. His teaching was positive and active, while theirs was negative and passive. Confucius counselled: 'Do not to others what you would not wish done to yourself.' Rabbi Hillel put it: 'What is hateful to thee, do not to anyone else.' Their teaching smacked of calculated prudence. Jesus's teaching was active benevolence.

It is easier not to do certain things, say injure a person, than to do something positive. Mere inaction will achieve the former, but it takes firm resolve to say, 'I will go out of my way to be as kind and helpful to others as I would wish them to be to me.' To observe this principle means more than avoiding wrongdoing. It involves making our neighbour's concerns our own, loving him as we love ourselves, and treating him as magnanimously as God has treated us. This is high ground.

But this principle does not stand by itself, for man has a duty to God as well as to his neighbour. Loving our fellow man, good and necessary though it is, is no substitute for loving God with all our heart and mind. 'These ought ye also to have done, and not to have left the other undone' (Matt. 23 : 23) were the Master's words.

This standard is so exacting that no man can carry it out fully and exhibit it in his life in his own unaided strength. It is not the product of mere human resolve and endeavour. Only one who has received new life from God through new birth can come within cooee of achieving its demands. The dynamic for obedience must be supplied from outside his fallen nature, and, thank God, that dynamic is available.

1. Lees, *The King's Way*, p. 93.

2. See E. G. Carre, *Praying Hyde* (London, Pickering and Inglis), p. 136.

3. Hunter, *Design for Life*, p. 84.

4. Lees, op. cit., p. 106.

5. Jamieson, Faussett and Brown, *Commentary*, p. 910.

12

The Solemnity of Human Choice

Matthew 7 : 13–29

Many commentators consider that the Sermon really ends with 7 : 12, and that the remaining verses are an epilogue with concluding warning and appeal.

When unfolding the spiritual principles on which His Kingdom was based, Jesus was at pains to make it clear that discipleship was costly, and that there was no such thing as 'cheap grace'. Self-sacrifice and self-denial were part and parcel of the life of the Kingdom. But He was equally careful to assure His hearers that this was the path to true blessedness.

Some time later He taught the same truth in terms of the disciple taking up his cross and bearing it after Him—a rather forbidding prospect. But as Samuel Rutherford happily expressed it, 'Whoso looketh on the white side of Christ's cross and taketh it up hand-somely, will find it just such a burden as wings are to a bird.'

The crowds were listening in as Jesus unburdened His heart to His disciples, for verses 28 and 29 record 'that the people were astonished at His doctrine, for He taught them as one having authority and not as the scribes'. The warnings and appeals of this section would have special relevance to their spiritual condition and

147

needs. If they were inclined to enter the strait gate and walk the narrow way, better that they should realise at the beginning that it is not the most popular way. The very idea of a gate presupposes restrictions.

In John 14:6 G. Campbell Morgan sees a striking parallel with verses 13 and 14. Here are his words:

> Said Jesus on another occasion to men—and the words flash their light upon this passage—'I am the way, and the truth, and the life.' 'Enter ye in by the narrow gate and find the true way, for I am the Way.' Beware of false prophets . . . but listen to the true Prophet, Who is Essential Truth for 'I am the Truth'; and walk in comradeship with Him upon the way, having come to Him for entrance to the Kingdom. Do not depend upon what you do but upon what you are . . . Trust only to the fact that you are in yourself, as He was in Himself—conditioned in the will of God, for 'I am the Life'.[1]

It was because the narrow way with all its apparent limitations and restrictions led to life—begun now and to be consummated later—that Jesus urged His hearers to enter the strait gate and tread the narrow way. Not that He was a kill-joy, but He knew that the broad way led to irreparable loss and ruin, to 'destruction'; that was why He was so urgent in His plea to leave the broad way and enter the gate which leads to life.

Throughout the whole section Jesus presents in a series of vivid contrasts the truth He is imparting. There are two gates, the wide and the strait; two ways, the broad and the narrow; two destinations, life and destruction; two groups of travellers, many and few; two trees, good and corrupt; two kinds of fruit, good and bad; two builders, wise and foolish; two foundations, rock and sand; two houses, and two issues of the storm. It would be impossible to depict more graphically the solemnity of the decision His hearers must make. In this model

Sermon Jesus preaches for a verdict, and like a master-craftsman, builds up to a tremendous climax which appeals alike to intellect and emotions and will.

TWO WAYS OF LIFE

> Enter by the narrow gate, for the gate is wide, and the way is broad that leads to destruction, and many are those who enter it. For the gate is small, and the way is narrow that leads to life, and few are those who find it (vv. 13, 14 N.A.S.V.).

Note first that the narrow gate is not the gate to heaven, as some have supposed. It is the entrance to the way that leads to life. It would appear that entering this gate signifies the beginning of Christian experience, or conversion, which is the necessary prelude to entering the Kingdom of God. Entering the wide gate, then, would be the choice of the world with its obvious allurements rather than the Kingdom with its apparent restrictions and disciplines. Jesus challenges His hearers to make a crucial choice.

The broad way is so attractive to those who tread it, because they are free to do exactly what they like, to go their own way. It is the way of self-indulgence and indiscipline.

A West Indian who had chosen Mohammedanism in preference to Christianity, gave as his reason that 'Mohammedanism is a noble, broad path—there is room for a man and his sins on it. The way of Christ is a narrow way—the sins have to be left behind.' Just so.

The small gate and the narrow way smack of self-sacrifice and self-denial, and this is not welcome to the man whose interests are worldly and materialistic. The life of one who walks the narrow way is defined in the Beatitudes, and they are the portion only of the spiritual man.

There is another contrast. The small gate is not easy to pass through, for Jesus said elsewhere, 'Strive to enter in at the strait gate' (Luke 13:24). It is a strenuous life from the beginning, and involves moral effort. It begins with conflict, for the evil one will not be inactive when the choice is being made. The conflict is often fierce. While it is not all glamour, the end is glorious.

But though entry may be difficult and involves repentance and self-abasement, the narrow way on the far side of the gate is in reality an ever-broadening one, leading on to light and life, eternal and abundant. This life is the enjoyment of mystical union with Christ, sharing His very life here and hereafter.

On the other hand, the wide gate, though easy to enter, and the broad way, though alluring at first, is ever-narrowing, until it ushers the traveller into the narrow defile of 'destruction', which begins now and is climaxed in eternal separation from God. Then how solemn is the choice involved. The doctrine of the two ways indicates how crucial are the choices made in this life.

The question naturally arises from the Lord's words 'many' and 'few' in this connection, whether this indicates that the vast bulk of mankind will be lost. The best answer to this question is that given by the Master: 'Someone said to Him, "Lord, are there just a few who are being saved?" And He said to them, "Strive to enter by the narrow door, for many, I tell you, will seek to enter and will not be able . . ."' (Luke 13:23–4 N.A.S.V.).

> To every man there openeth
> A way and ways and a way;
> And the high soul treads the high way,
> And the low soul gropes the low;
> And in between on the misty flats
> The rest drift to and fro;
> But to every man there openeth

A high way and a low,
And every man decideth
The way his soul shall go.

John Oxenham

Jesus refused to be drawn on a problem which was purely speculative, and which was not the business of the one who put the question. That is God's province. Where Jesus with His full knowledge gave no definite reply to satisfy mere curiosity, we have even more reason to follow His example, since we have no basis of knowledge.

TWO TYPES OF TEACHER

Beware of false prophets, which come to you in sheep's clothing, but inwardly they are ravening wolves. Ye shall know them by their fruits. Do men gather grapes of thorns, or figs of thistles? Even so, every good tree bringeth forth good fruit, but a corrupt tree bringeth forth evil fruit. A good tree cannot bring forth evil fruit, neither can a corrupt tree bring forth good fruit. Every tree that bringeth not forth good fruit is hewn down, and cast into the fire. Wherefore by their fruits ye shall know them (vv. 15–20).

In these words Jesus warned prospective travellers on the narrow way that all their troubles would not be over when they entered the strait gate. There would be false prophets who would seek to deflect them from the path that leads to life. They speak fair-sounding words, but their characters belie their teaching.

In all ages deceptive leaders have crept into the Church, and never have they been so numerous or so subtle as today. Professing to guide and feed the flock of God, instead, they bring in 'damnable heresies'. Their proselytising zeal is fantastic. Their outward appearance is not calculated to arouse suspicion, for they wear 'sheep's clothing'. Eastern shepherds often wore sheepskins with the wool next their skin. But it is possible to wear a sheepskin without being a sheep! The Lord is here giving a sharp warning against the peril of hypocrisy and proselytising.

The test of the true prophet is conformity to the Scriptures in his teaching and conformity to the character and teaching of Christ in his life. The false teacher with his attractive personality and plausible manner easily insinuates himself into the favour of the flock. But though he poses as an innocent sheep, inwardly he is a ravenous wolf. His words are honeyed, but their real purpose is carefully concealed. In him, the devil works as an angel of light.

How is the traveller to distinguish the true prophet from the false? Twice in this passage Jesus gives the test, 'By their fruits ye shall know them', and He illustrates His point from two trees, one good, and the other corrupt. The test of a tree is the quality of its fruit. A corrupt tree cannot produce good fruit, and vice versa.

Fruit here includes teaching as well as practice, and in this context the emphasis is on the latter. The crucial questions to be answered are: 'Does his teaching harmonise with Scripture?' 'Is his character in keeping with the principles of the Sermon as taught and exemplified by Christ?' A Christ-like character is the product of the Holy Spirit's activity, and manifests itself in the fruit of the spirit (Gal. 5:22–3). Where such a character is absent, striking miracles and brilliant successes are of no significance. The end of the corrupt tree is to be cut down.

Jesus adds a further solemn warning:

Many will say to me in that day, Lord, Lord, have we not prophesied in Thy name? and in Thy name have cast out devils? and in Thy name done many wonderful works? And then I will profess to them, I never knew you. Depart from me, ye that work iniquity (vv. 21–2).

One striking fact emerges from this paragraph. Jesus here tacitly and solemnly assumes, as the Son of God, His position as Judge of all men. In this office He warns that these hypocritical false prophets will in that day have the sheep's clothing torn away and their true nature will be exposed. The criterion of judgment then will be, not preaching and teaching and miracles, but doing the will of God. Spectacular performances and even alleged miracles do not necessarily imply divine authentication. More is required than mere lip-profession.

The word 'knew' in the fateful sentence, 'I never knew you', means 'to know with favour, or to acknowledge'. One writer suggests that the statement means, 'Our acquaintance was not broken off—there never was any. They claimed intimacy. Jesus will deny that any intimacy ever existed.' How solemn the verdict, 'Depart from me!'

TWO TYPES OF FOUNDATION

Therefore, whosoever heareth these sayings of mine, and doeth them, I will liken him unto a wise man which built his house upon a rock: And the rain descended and the floods came, and the winds blew, and beat upon that house; and it fell not: for it was founded upon a rock. And everyone that heareth these sayings of mine and doeth them not, shall be likened unto a foolish man, which built his house upon the sand; and the rain descended, and the floods came, and the winds blew and beat upon that house; and it fell: and great was the fall of it (vv. 24–7).

'It is the consciousness that the Speaker is nothing less than the final Judge of all which makes the parable of the builders on the rock and the sand, with which the sermon closes, the most solemn and overpowering of all the words of Jesus.' So wrote James Denney.[2]

The words are addressed specifically to the whole assembled crowd: '*Whosoever* heareth . . . *Everyone* that heareth . . .' Each of us is a builder, building the house of our life by the thoughts we think, the words we speak, the actions we perform. Each builds on either stable rock or shifting sand. Each of us is either wise or foolish. Each house either stands or falls in the testing hour. Such are the antitheses with which the Lord confronts us all.

In building the house of our life the supremely important thing is not the materials incorporated into the superstructure, but the stability of the foundation on which it rests. The external appearance of the house is no criterion of its ability to endure. During the long dry season the house built on sand appears as stable as that built on rock. The crucial difference becomes evident when the storms beat upon them.

And come the storms assuredly will; storms that will test to the limit the foundation to which our life has been anchored. If we have built upon the shifting sands of ever-changing science, or of humanism, or of materialism, or of status and success, it is built upon sand. When the rains of testing fall and the floods of tragedy, bereavement, temptation or persecution rise and overwhelm us, the house we have constructed will collapse in ruins—because it was founded on sand.

If, on the other hand, the master-principle of our life has been hearing and doing 'these sayings of mine', Jesus says we have built on immovable rock. Our life is anchored to Christ, 'and other foundation can no man lay, than that is laid, which is Jesus Christ' (1 Cor. 3 : 11). Equally severe storms will beat upon this house, but it will stand impregnable, because founded on the rock.

The secret of security and stability is a character built upon the Person and Work of our Lord Jesus Christ. 'No spiritual fabric that is built on anything else than the teaching of the Son of Man can endure the strain and the stress which will come upon it before the end.'[3] The storm reveals the quality of the life.

The outcome of the test is a matter of supreme importance. Of the house erected by the wise man, we read that 'it fell not'. But of the house built by the foolish man it is recorded, 'it fell, and great was the fall of it'.

With these solemn words Jesus brought His incomparable Sermon to a close. He preached for a verdict. What is your response? Are you a wise or a foolish builder?

> On Christ, the solid rock, I stand,
> All other ground is sinking sand.
>
> E. Mote

1. G. Campbell Morgan, *The Gospel of Matthew*, p. 76.
2. James Denney, *Jesus and His Gospel* (London, Hodder and Stoughton), p. 251.
3. Gore, *The Sermon on the Mount*, p. 175.

13

The Spirit's Dynamic for Achievement

Matthew 7 : 11; Luke 11:13

The amazing Sermon has concluded. The crowds, astonished at its content, and the authority with which it was delivered, melt away (vv. 28, 29). Now they must face up to the challenge with which they have been confronted and make their individual choice—as must we. What was their reaction? More important, what is our reaction?

To a thoughtful, spiritually sensitive person, the lofty ideals, the wonderful spiritual principles of the Sermon could not but make a deep impression. All that was best in him would respond to its tremendous appeal. But the very loftiness of its standards leaves us all longing but hopeless. Like Alexander Whyte, we feel that the groan of Romans 7 is the logical outcome of our study. Instead of presenting a glowing incentive, some see the Sermon as a distant glistening, snowy peak—glorious but quite unscalable, because they discern in it no power for fulfilment.

This very impression was voiced by Dean Strong when he said, 'The Sermon on the Mount gives no word as to the way of realising the perfection it preaches; it still remains a law.'

But not every one views it thus. Herbert Snell

affirmed, 'If I get close to the Sermon on the Mount, I see there the shadow of the cross on every page.' Just as the Law was 'a schoolmaster to lead us to Christ', so the Sermon is a stimulus to drive us to the cross which was not far in the future when it was preached.

To some members of his congregation who complained that his teaching on the Sermon on the Mount was faulty because 'it was not preaching the gospel', Joseph Parker replied: 'There is nothing evangelic, there is nothing doctrinally savoury, there is no old wine of blood? Seneca might have said this, it might have been written in old Latin? You think so? You try to carry out the injunction of the text, and ere you have gone two steps in the direction of its accomplishment, you will want Christ and the cross, and the blood, and the Holy Ghost.'

CAN THE IDEAL BE REALISED?

Is it really true that the Sermon 'gives no word as to the way of realising the perfection it preaches'? Further study and reflection will reveal that this is not the case.

Consider first the context of the Sermon as a whole. It must not be divorced from the One who preached and exemplified it, or from the setting in which it is placed by divine inspiration. It does not stand by itself. It follows the facts and teaching recorded in chapters 1–4. Matthew is considered to be the most orderly of the gospel writers in the presentation of his material.

In chapters 1–4 Matthew records the incarnation of God in a Christ who was truly human (1:25) and yet really divine (1:23). The teaching of the Sermon comes from this God-man to whom all power in heaven and on earth was committed. Matthew recounts our Lord's temptation, and shows that the secret of His victory lay in His being filled with the Spirit (4:1; Luke 4:14), and being filled with the Word (4:4, 7, 10 cf. Eph. 5:18 ff. and Col. 3:16 ff.). The human, tempted Christ points the way to victory. Does this have no bearing on what follows?

And what of its subsequent context? It is immediately followed by three miracles of power, miracles which are illuminating parables to those conscious of their inadequacy and insufficiency in the light of such impossible demands. He healed the leper of his uncleanness (8 : 3). He imparted power to the impotent paralytic (8 : 13). He dispelled the fever which disabled Peter's mother-in-law for effective service (8 : 14, 15). Immediately after the searching words of Jesus came these mighty works of Jesus, to encourage us to believe that He who commanded would also enable us to translate His ideals into personal experience.

Nowhere did Jesus indicate that the Sermon was the whole of the gospel. It was the manifesto of His Kingdom. The great facts which constitute the Good News had yet to be enacted. Bethlehem and the Incarnation demonstrated that a holy life could be lived on earth. Calvary and the atonement satisfied God's demands and removed man's guilt. Easter and the resurrection confirmed the acquittal and released resurrection life. Pentecost and the gift of the Spirit provided the needed dynamic for fulfilment.

SHOULD WE PRAY FOR THE SPIRIT?

It must be admitted that, divorced from Pentecost, the standards of the Sermon are frankly impossible to failing men and women as we are. But it is not divorced from Pentecost as we shall see.

Notice that the 'good things' of Matt. 7 : 11 are interpreted to us in the parallel passage in Luke 11 : 13 as 'the Holy Spirit'. All the 'good things' our heavenly Father promises to give us are wrapped up in 'the Holy Spirit'. This is a very important and significant fact.

'If you then being evil know how to give good gifts to your children, how much more shall your heavenly

Father give the Holy Spirit to those who ask Him' (Luke 11:13 N.A.S.V.). This verse has been a problem to some. In the light of the gift of the Holy Spirit on the Day of Pentecost they see no validity in it for the believer today. Why pray, they say, for what has already been bestowed. C. I Scofield follows this line: 'It is evident that none of the disciples, with the possible exception of Mary of Bethany, asked for the Spirit in the faith of this promise . . . To go back to the promise of Luke 11:13 is to forget Pentecost, and to ignore the truth that now every believer has the indwelling Spirit.'[1]

But is this necessarily so? If it is, then this verse had application for only the few weeks between the time when it was spoken and the Day of Pentecost, a most unlikely circumstance, since in the Sermon Jesus was enunciating eternal principles.

A flood of light is shed on the problem, however, by a statement of H. B. Swete, one of the greatest authorities on the doctrine of the Holy Spirit. He points out that the definite article, 'the Holy Spirit', is omitted fifty-four times and inserted thirty-four times. When it is present, it refers to the Holy Spirit as a Person. When it is omitted, the reference is to the gifts and operations of the Holy Spirit on our behalf. *In Luke 11:13 the definite article is omitted*. So what Jesus was encouraging His hearers to do was not to pray the Father for the gift of the Holy Spirit as a Person, but to pray for the special gifts or operations of the Spirit which they needed for the fulfilment of the will of God, and the discharge of their responsibilities in the Body of Christ. Here, it seems, is the solution to the problem.

What a wealth of promise this brings within the grasp of 'those who *ask* Him'! True, we no longer need to ask for the Holy Spirit as a divine indwelling Person, but we *may* and *should* and *must* ask and keep on asking the Father, confidently, for the very operation of the Spirit we stand in need of at the moment in life and service. It is in the context of such importunate prayer that this verse stands, with the six-times repeated assurance of an answer (7 : 7–8).

If this wonderful Sermon with its stupendous demands is to be increasingly translated into personal experience, what do we need? It can be met by the appropriate operation of the Holy Spirit.

Is it *power* for the demands of the day or the exigencies of service? He is the Spirit of *power* (2 Tim. 1 : 7). Is it wisdom we lack? He is the Spirit of *wisdom* (Isa. 11 : 2). Do we long for graciousness? He is the Spirit of *grace* (Heb. 10 : 29). Is it purity we need? He is the Spirit of *holiness* (Rom. 1 : 4). Do we fail in the realm of prayer? He is the Spirit of *supplication* (Zech. 12 : 10). Are we in the grip of a critical spirit? He is the Spirit of *love* (Rom. 5 : 5). Whatever we need for holy living and fruitful service, the Holy Spirit will be that to us for the asking.

Ponder the promise : 'How *much more* will your heavenly Father give the Holy Spirit to them that *ask* Him.' What more can God give than Himself, and all the resources of Deity? Then let us ask and keep on asking as our needs arise. 'God opens to us the resources of His own nature for the realising of the perfection He demands.'

On his first visit to the English Keswick Convention, Dr J. Elder Cumming, a Scottish divine who later became one of the regular speakers there, was very prejudiced. After two days he was still very critical and said to an Edinburgh theological professor, 'There is nothing more in this teaching than in the Shorter Catechism.' Though tempted to go home, he remained till the end. When the Convention closed, his whole soul was aflame. He said to the same professor, 'My brother, these men have combined the great white Sermon on the Mount with Pentecost, and made it possible.' Let us each do the same.

1. *The Scofield Reference Bible*, p. 1090.